BIRDS IN
Love

JEAN LÉVEILLÉ

Voyageur Press

EDICATION

For my companion, Denise, whose invaluable help and unfailing support sustain me.

CKNOWLEDGEMENTS

My thanks to Les Éditions de l'Homme, My-Trang Nguyen, Monique C. Cleland, and Amy Rost for their help with this book.

First published in 2007 by Voyageur Press, an imprint of MBI Publishing Company, Galtier Plaza, Suite 200, 380 Jackson Street, St. Paul, MN 55101 USA

Text copyright © 2007 by Jean Léveillé
Photographs copyright © 2007 by Jean Léveillé, except where noted

Translation of *Les oiseaux et l'amour*
First published in French by Les Éditions de l'Homme
© Les Éditions de l'Homme, 2003
Les Éditions de l'Homme is a division of Groupe Sogides Inc.

Photographs on pages 2, 4 (top right, lower right, and left), 7, 10, 12, 35 (lower left), 37, 38, 54, 57 (lower), 62, 64 (lower), 66, 74, 77, 82, 84, 86 (top), 87 (top), 96, 116, 118, 124, 126 (lower right), 127 (lower), 131, 132, 133, 134, 137 (top), 142, 146, 159 (lower) are from Shutterstock.

MBI Publishing Company titles are also available at discounts in bulk quantity for industrial or sales-promotional use. For details write to Special Sales Manager at MBI Publishing Company, Galtier Plaza, Suite 200, 380 Jackson Street, St. Paul, MN 55101 USA

Library of Congress Cataloging-in-Publication Data
Léveillé, Jean.
 [Les oiseaux et l'amour. English]
 Birds in love : the secret courting & mating rituals of extraordinary birds / by Jean Léveillé.
   p. cm.
 ISBN-13: 978-0-7603-2807-1 (plc w/ jacket)
 ISBN-10: 0-7603-2807-2 (plc w/ jacket)
 1. Birds--Behavior. 2. Courtship in animals. I. Title.
QL698.3.L4813 2007
598.156--dc22

                    2007011532

Translated and adapted from the French by My-Trang Nguyen
Additional translation by Monique C. Cleland
Editor: Amy Rost
Cover Designer: Brenda C. Canales

Interior Designer: Maria Friedrich

Printed in China

Contents

THE MEMORIES OF LONG LOVE
GATHER LIKE DRIFTING SNOW,
POIGNANT AS THE MANDARIN DUCKS,
WHO FLOAT SIDE BY SIDE IN SLEEP.

—Lady Murasaki Shikibu, *The Tale of Genji*
Translated from the Japanese by Arthur Waley

INTRODUCTION

When still just a boy, I was fascinated by a mysterious and melodious song that rang out through the stillness of the evening: "Old Sam Peabody, Peabody, Peabody...," it seemed to say. The singer turned out to be a pretty little white-throated sparrow looking—in vain, apparently—for a mate. Even more moving was the haunting, languorous daybreak supplications made by a pair of common loons eager for romance.

The years slipped by, and life's daily concerns temporarily erased those vibrant songsters from my memory bank. Then romance came knocking at my own door, and with it, a patient companion who also loved to observe—not to mention identify and classify—those feathered creatures. Denise and I became an inseparable bird-watching pair; "us" and "we" eventually supplanted "me" and "I" as we set out to discover this often misunderstood but always fascinating world of "identified flying objects."

We redesigned our garden just for the birds' enjoyment, tempting them with irresistible shrubs, fruit trees, and fancy feeders. Soon enough, they came calling—those we couldn't identify as well as the more familiar varieties. The natives became regular visitors to our neighborhood, while rarer creatures, nomads, and other objects of curiosity were occasional delights. And we traveled to the backyards of other species, often located in the far-flung corners of the globe. There, we met other keen and experienced fellow birders with whom we exchanged secrets and discoveries.

Consulting specialized books and using increasingly sophisticated equipment, we improved our identification skills, in particular the ability to decipher the birds' often baffling mating patterns. Now we know, for instance, that a cry of alarm, a territorial song, and a mating call are all differently modulated, depending upon time and place. As I try to get to know the birds more intimately, I'm surprised by my own facility in recognizing various behaviors and characteristics. Now I can differentiate the infinite variations in their plumage, their tremulous vocal inflections, the choreographic patterns that accompany their short-lived though frequently complex encounters.

What is the point of those amazingly varied courting stages, of the delicate manners males employ so as not to alarm the females? Why do cranes keep on fine-tuning their elegant dances, and common loons modulate their haunting laughter? Why all those nuptial rituals?

Questions like these inevitably prompted us to examine the close connection between humans and birds—love, just love, as the old song goes, something that generations of poets have written about, set to music, and ardently pursue. Did we really invent the subtle devices we commonly use to pursue or court the object of our desires? Or were we inspired over the ages by the obvious and subtle attentions that birds display to one another? The questions and assumptions are endless, and as yet we have few answers. And that fact gives us many more delightful hours of observation.

A peahen gives her beloved a kiss.

Tree swallows make love perched on a high wire.

PURPLE-THROATED CARIBS

Early one morning in the Antilles, we left our sandy beach and the "flip flop" sound of the turquoise waters to drive along a narrow winding road that led us into the hills. There we found a beautiful garden owned by a very nice bird-loving old lady. Not only did she cultivate flowers of all sorts, but she also provided feeders for her feathered friend, the purple-throated carib. As she welcomed us, we could already see one of these hummingbirds flipping his wings over a fluffy red flower.

In this Garden of Eden, we spent hours watching a male and female carib as they drank from feeders and flowers and chased each other in pursuits that, to our eyes, seemed friendly enough. (The sexes were distinguishable because the female's beak is slightly longer and more curved than the male's.) What alluring and elusive creatures those tiny, deep purple hummers were! Their customs and behavior are usually almost impossible to observe, as are their rather unusual breeding habits.

Come spring, the self-absorbed male—polygamous by nature—obsessively pursues as many prospects as he can manage to attract. He rehearses his nuptial dance—repeatedly flying high, then swooping back down in a swift arc—dazzling them all, each in turn, with a spectacular display of his brilliant, iridescent plumage.

Few females can resist such sparkling come-ons. As it happens, many willingly succumb to the

Facing page:
A male purple-throated carib will suck dry the flowers that border his territory. Females, thinking the area devoid of food, must then venture into his private property. There, he lets them feast on his flowers—in exchange for sexual favors.

Below:
The carib's brilliant, iridescent plumage glints in the sun as he pauses to rest.

dandy's charms and gallant courtship. But the foppish male's extravagant passion amounts to little more than a one-night stand. After copulation, the seducer promptly takes off, discarding any notion of parental responsibility and leaving the female to cope with the mundane tasks of building a nest, incubating their eggs, and rearing their offspring. Rare are the male procreators who hang around or offer to incubate the eggs—elliptical and always white—even for short interludes. Worry-free, the commitment-shy Romeo flies on to fresh conquests.

Photographing and observing our pair in the garden, we realized that the male was preparing to do just that by aggressively staking out a vast feeding territory. These caribs, like all hummingbirds, have copious gizzards, and the males regularly patrol the area bordering their turf, sucking the flowers dry and thereby putting out the word that the entire domain has been emptied of nectar.

Hungry, foraging often in vain, and with their young clamoring for food, desperate mothers, like the female we were watching, succumb to trespassing on the rascal's private property. And there—surprise, surprise—they discover that food is still abundant. After many attempts, they finally get a pass, allowing them to stock up—in return, of course, for sexual favors on every visit. The age-old barter system is alive and well in the kingdom of the birds.

But when you think about it, what choice do these mothers really have? As in some other societies, they volunteer to sell their bodies rather than allow their offspring to suffer. Single parenthood is taxing and exhausting. The mothers have only themselves to rely on if they need a brief respite or moment of relaxation.

While the purple-throated caribs' sexual behavior may not always be politically correct, these fragile but magnificent miniature species deserve to be cared for by loving hands, like those of our frail host. After thanking her, we went back to our small rented car and drove down the hill with mixed feelings. We appreciated every moment of this day, but we couldn't help but wonder who would take over the garden—and maintain the home for the little purple lovers—after the old lady passed away.

CHARACTERISTICS

Purple-throated carib (*Eulampis jugularis*): Male and female identical; $4^{1}/2$ inches (11 to 12 cm), slightly curved bill; back, head, and abdomen velvety black; throat and chest lush purple; brilliant golden-green wings. **Distribution:** West Indies

From the front, the carib's eponymous purple throat is clearly visible.

TREE SWALLOWS

The tree swallows are always the first to return to our back yard in Montreal after the winter. Some are breathless after the long journey north from Venezuela, others are more relaxed, having wintered over stateside. All exuberantly spread the good news of imminent spring.

Before long, couples check out the old nest boxes we patiently repainted during the long hibernation season. They flick in and out of the manmade structures, circle some before alighting on an electric wire, where they look like tiny notes on a sheet of music.

After a sometimes long and harsh Quebec winter, spring comes as the promise of a new life, and the charming, vivacious swallows are nature's gift to this new season. Near our home is a quaint little park where we like to go and watch them flirt as they perch together on the sun-dappled hemp ropes.

Soon they begin the lengthy grooming of their steel blue-green plumage. Lovers' rituals are punctuated by much greeting and bowing; one partner precariously leans forward to peck its significant other amid a concert of song and a rustling of wings. Euphoric, the male flutters about, beats his wings and twitters before attempting the gesture that could either spell consummation or put an end to it all: he perches atop his beloved's back, delicately nipping at her neck feathers for balance and stability. If she is receptive, the female simply goes along. From time to time, though, she objects to the male's advance, not yet ready to go all the way. She spreads her wings to signal reluctance, delaying the ultimate act for later, if not rejecting it altogether.

The reaction is common among immature females, who are easily spotted by their dark-hued upper parts, sometimes tinged with brown or gray. Abandoned and homeless, they exist on the fringe of tree swallow society, with nowhere to go except, perhaps, the nest of a more assertive sister. But that's by no means a safe haven. The incensed sister may ruthlessly chase an immature female away or kill her in a violent fit of rage.

Barely distinguishable from the males, mature female tree swallows betray themselves by their habit of coiling up in a Y during moments of ecstasy. And so the lovers carry on predictably and uneventfully until one gray, gloomy morning when they vanish without a trace. Days pass before they reappear, as suddenly as the sun, resuming their task of assembling rootlets, stalks, and twigs.

CHARACTERISTICS

Tree swallow (*Tachycineta bicolor*): Only swallow with greenish glints; throat and abdomen white; Y-shaped tail. Sings with distinct, fluid notes. **Distribution**: North America

Facing page:
A loving couple exchanges sweet nothings.

Nest building is the expectant mother's domain, and her weakness for white-feathered lining knows no bounds. The male's job is to find the raw material. The prudent ones go straight to the source, chasing ducks and gulls; the more careless raid their neighbors' nests at the last minute, sometimes risking their own lives in the ensuing battles. But then the first egg appears and, as if by magic, all struggles and tensions dissipate. Once the four to six white eggs are well ensconced in their warm down bed, the mother confidently takes off with her lover. They're gone for days on end—two to four to be exact. As to where they go and what they are up to, your guess is as good as mine. Then it is back home, hunting insects and living the everyday life of a swallow family.

Those endearing little birds are an illustration of love and the symbol of nature's annual rebirth in our northern country.

After much flirting, a male tree swallow perches atop his receptive lover's back, delicately nipping at her neck feathers for balance and stability.

The return of the tree swallow to northern climes also hails the return of spring—and mating season.

The newlywed tree swallows set up house in a manmade swallow box, where the female assembles the nest from the stalks and twigs the male brings. She lines the nest with copious amount of white down, the better to cushion her little ones.

White-throated and White-crowned Sparrows

It all began casually enough: a plant here, a shrub there, and before we knew it, Denise and I had created an oasis in the midst of the bustling city. In our back yard, lush flora abounds, attracting an increasing variety of birds, both local and from away. How they manage to find our paradise is beside the point, but on this sweet spring morning, as sweet as only the month of May can deliver, the surprise is enchanting.

We can spot white-throated sparrows, for instance, foraging side by side with a few white-crowned sparrows, their cousins, brought here perhaps by sheer coincidence, a contrary wind, a premature change of season, or even the still vivid memories of a long-ago, ardent springtime romance. The dinner menu, meant for one flock, will have to suit both.

And how they sing! "Old Sam Peabody, Peabody, Peabody..." they chirp, enlivening the already brilliant garden. Such clear, quavering whistles, sustained by a rush of staccato riffs. A clear and powerful voice rings out from inside the bushes, ranging through the entire repertoire of nuptial songs. Before long, the singer can be heard practicing one bar at a time, repeating the notes over and over, as if rehearsing for one final and triumphant encounter.

All male white-throats—whether carefree bachelors, widowers, or dignified patriarchs—love to sing. Besides foraging, they devote their brief stay on our patio to fine-tuning their vocal chords and practicing other seduction techniques. After all, when it comes to the art of love, no male can afford to leave anything to chance. The easily distracted female requires more than just the familiar "Peabody" tune, however thrilling it may sound to human ears.

But there's little point in having an exquisite voice if one's plumage doesn't quite make the grade. So a dashing nuptial costume is also in the cards, and it is crucial to flaunt one's lustrous whites, yellows, and browns during courtship. From the female's point of view, a chic costume is proof of its wearer's masculinity, of his ability to stake out and defend a territory abundant enough to feed their brood. A less elegant individual might have to make do with a scraggly patch of land, devoid of fatty, nutritious insects.

And so year in, year out, even the most experienced suitor keeps an eye on his chums, those flashy young upstarts who will stop at nothing in their quest for a mate. The less flamboyant among them—often neophytes—

CHARACTERISTICS

White-crowned sparrow (*Zonotrichia leucophrys*): Crown striped with black and white; pinkish beak; clear gray breast. **Distribution**: North America, Cuba, Gulf Coast of Mexico

White-throated sparrow (*Zonotrichia albicollis*). Well-defined white throat; yellow spot between beak and eye; head striped with black and white. **Distribution**: North America

Facing page:
To court a female, the male white-throated sparrow sports lustrous white and brown plumage, accented with yellow. For the female, such a chic costume proves the wearer's masculinity.

hardly stand a chance and must resign themselves to yet another year among the ranks of the lonely hearts. Such is the implacable truth about love and conquest in the realm of the white-throats: scruffy plumage, an unflattering light, and you're out of luck.

White-crowns, on the other hand, pay little heed to their appearance. Yet birders generally find them more attractive than their white-throated cousins and their song less strident. They're slightly larger than the white-throats, sport paler-looking bills—pinkish or yellowish—and have a crown striped with black and white. Their face, neck, and breast are dressed in various shades of gray.

The flock of white-crowns winters on the immense plains of the southern and midwestern United States, returning each spring to their breeding grounds in the northern climes. Social standing is determined by each bird's vocal timbre, as is success or failure in courtship. And so they sing, forever practicing their melody, perfecting their pitch, all in the hope of meeting that special someone, of winning over the object of their desire.

The chance encounters between these bird cousins intrigue us birders. Those stray white-crowns mysteriously turn up among the white-throats from time to time, and we wait for the ensuing romances and look forward to stories of their hybrid offspring. Born of those elegant throats and gorgeous crowns, these crossbreeds promise endless new songs and unfamiliar dialects.

The white-throated sparrow and the white-crowned sparrow are really cousins, and they share most of the same parental behaviors. In both species, it is the female who builds the nest and incubates the eggs. But since the two species' breeding ranges are in different regions, they use different nesting material. The white-throated female uses coarse grass, conifer needles, and twigs to build a cup-shaped nest on the ground, at the base of a bush or a conifer. The white-crowned female also builds her nest on the ground, but because she lives in a northern region, she uses lichen and moss and prefers to line the nest with grasses, hair, or ptarmigan feathers. After hatching of the eggs, both parents of the two species feed the young until they can manage by themselves.

A male white-throated sparrow dressed up in plumage to go a-courting.

Male white-crowned sparrows may be more striking and colorful than their white-throated cousins, but their songs are less strident. His vocal timbre determines a male white-crown's social standing.

AFRICAN JACANAS

The characteristic golden chest and blue frontal patch are clearly visible on this African jacana.

CHARACTERISTICS

African jacana (*Actophilornis Africana*): Long legs and toes; blue frontal patch; neck white in front, black in back; golden-colored chest; rest of body reddish brown. **Distribution**: Sub-Saharan Africa

Kenya is a beautiful country with amazing nature, and for me, the best way to appreciate it is to set up a small tent amid the vegetation, the animals, and the birds. The camping ground on the shores of Lake Baringo was idyllic, with its luxurious vegetation, big centennial trees, monkeys, gazelles, hippos, crocodiles, lions, and birds, birds, birds. On the lake, among the water lilies, the jacanas were very busy. Denise and I were having a very good time watching them, while at the same time we kept an eye on the monkeys high in the trees above.

The African jacana is one species in a small family of shorebirds. Jacanas owe their name to the Tupi Indians of Brazil, and their originality to a rather stark reversal of traditional roles, not to mention polyandry.

The larger and physically stronger female jacana is the dominant, aggressive partner, given to defending her territory against female intruders, chasing them away relentlessly. Just watch her wings: if they lift straight up, the lady is mad as hell!

The male of the species is left to play Mister Mom.

First, during the rainy season—when watercourses and marshes teem with larvae and insects—he builds several floating platforms from aquatic plants. That accomplished, he invites the female over for a visit. Playful cavorting ensues, in the form of heavy stomping by both partners. If the platform fails—and it often does—the couple promptly break up. If it holds, copulation takes place.

Only the steadiest and safest platform will be used as a nest, where the male alone incubates the eggs and generally looks after the young. He broods them when it's cold, leads them to foraging areas, scoops them up under his wings and flies them out of predators' reach, and so on. Thus occupied, he remains sexually inactive for at least 28 days and often for months on end.

From time to time, though, the stay-at-home dad might receive a visit from an ex-lover, eager to advise him about the future of his brood and, if necessary, even help him defend his own territory against an intruding female, her potential rival!

The polyandrous missus plays the field, dropping in on her multiple lovers—simultaneously or one at a time, depending on the circumstances. Copulating with four or five chums is par for the course—so much so that very few experts even bother to count them. But in the end, only a single individual will assume the responsibility of fatherhood.

Even the most attentive father cannot always prevent disaster in the jacanas' predator-infested wetlands. A cayman may float silently by, decimating the entire brood. If something like this happens, it's not uncommon to see the mother return to her mate and the pair resume their life together, if only long enough to produce a new clutch.

The sexual mores of jacanas are odd enough to attract the attention of experts for a long time to come. One can't help but wonder, for example, how the canny female manages to convince a male to look after a brood that belongs to another male bird. Is her loving attention toward her mate during breeding season enough to make him forget all her infidelities? Certainly for her, the ideal candidate for fatherhood is the one who can build the steadiest nesting platforms, capable of withstanding both water-level fluctuations and attacks by predators, and sufficiently well camouflaged to escape the prying eyes of birders—especially if they happen to be armed with a camera.

Like all jacana species, African jacanas favor wetland habitats.

A pair of African jacanas explores the shores of their home at Kenya's Lake Baringo.

Other Jacanas

The *Jacanidae* family consists of seven or eight species—experts haven't quite agreed on the precise number. I've been fortunate enough to encounter not only the African jacana, but also the bronze-winged jacana, the comb-crested jacana, and the northern jacana.

The bronze-winged jacana (*Metopidius indicus*) has a yellow beak and a large white band over its eyes. As its name implies, its back and wings are bronze, while its head, neck, and chest are black. Its frontal patch is barely visible. I photographed this beautiful bird in India; it is also native to Sumatra and Java.

We found comb-crested jacanas (*Irediparra gallinacea*) during a trip to northeastern Australia. Also found in Indonesia, the Philippines, and New Guinea, this species sports a bright pink crest, while its back and wings are dark brown. The chin and front of its neck are white, and its cheeks and lower neck are golden.

The northern jacana (*Jacana spinosa*) we saw in Costa Rica, where it is locally abundant. Its range is Mexico, Central America, and the West Indies. The northern jacana's neck, head, upper breast, and upper mantel are black, while the rest of the bird is chestnut brown. Its beak and frontal shield are bright yellow.

Like the African jacanas, the bronze wings, comb crests, and northerns favor wetland habitats, and they share the same unusual courtship and mating behaviors. They have the long legs and toes that are characteristic of all jacana species.

A bronze-winged jacana wades through its watery domain.

Long legs and toes are characteristics of all jacana species, including the comb-crested, seen here.

A male northern jacana sits on a nest. With all jacana species, the male plays Mister Mom, staying home and incubating the eggs—while the female is off cavorting with her other lovers.

DOUBLE-CRESTED CORMORANTS

After mating, the pair engages in some postcoital mutual grooming.

CHARACTERISTICS
Double-crested cormorant (*Phalacrocorax auritus*): 31$\frac{1}{2}$ inches (80 cm); predominantly black plumage, orange-yellow skin on face and throat; two rarely visible crests. **Distribution**: North America

We were bicycling in the land of mists and shadows. Long, thin, glittering veils of rain slid off our yellow, blue, and mauve raingear, as if gluing the three of us—our Chinese guide, my wife, and me—to the interminable wave of cyclists crisscrossing the Chinese countryside. Alerted by the squealing of our ancient bikes, a few peasants looked up, no doubt surprised to see Westerners in this remote corner of the globe. *"Ni hao, ni hao,"* we said, exchanging greetings.

Before long, we stopped beside the banks of a nearly black river. Flickering flames and lanterns dotted the darkened horizon, casting their doubles on the undulating surface of the water. Gradually we made out the silhouettes of cormorants and fishermen, both hard at work on the stream.

Mr. Mâ and his wife, Jade, our Chinese hosts during the four weeks we had been in the country, explained that the fishermen domesticate and train birds, usually great cormorants (*Phalacrocorax carbo*), to fish for them. The custom dates back to the end of the fourth century B.C. in China and continues today in China as well as Japan. The birds catch so many fish that the fishermen can feed their families and sell the surplus. It was a sight to behold, and treasure, for the age-old practice was on the wane.

Unfortunately, this fisherman's feathered partner no longer could put food on his table. After a life devoted to the fisherman, this cormorant was now too old to go fishing anymore.

To thank and honor his faithful bird, the fisherman prepared a great buffet of crustaceans and delectable fish, delicately laced with rice wine. Unused to eating and drinking so much, the bird fell asleep after this sumptuous meal, dying gently from the gastronomic excess. The end came peacefully. A brief ceremony followed, redolent of the mysterious East, committing the bird to earth.

At last it was reunited with its brave ancestors, hovering amid the curtains of fog.

Much has changed in China since our bicycle ride in the late 1980s. Nowadays few Chinese practice this kind of fishing, but our ageless fisherman still raises a few cormorants—not for work, but for the sole pleasure of watching them fall in love.

Originating in ancient Greece, the bird called *korax* or *korakos* eventually evolved into 29 species scattered across the planet. In the twelfth century, the Old French word *cormoreng* appeared, from which the English tongue derived its own *cormorant*. These days, cormorants have somewhat fallen from grace, accused of destroying the vegetation around their colony-nesting grounds. As a result, several countries have introduced measures restricting their breeding habits.

Most species—including North America's double-crested variety—sport predominantly black plumage. An appropriate light, however, will reveal dark blue or green reflections enhanced by tiny scales that adorn the feathers, those of the wings in particular.

But it's during the breeding season that the bird's transformation is most spectacular, even surreal, so much so that the entire colony goes absolutely berserk. Once, on a spring trip to Everglades National Park, I had the chance to observe this transformation. It was a beautiful sunny day, and I arrived very early, right when the park opened. To my astonishment, the birds, in all their breeding plumage splendor, were doing their courtship right in front of me, almost on the trail. It was a once-in-a-lifetime experience for a bird photographer, and I was thrilled.

The double-crested cormorant's courtship lasts a mere three to four weeks, during which a kaleidoscope of shimmering colors goes on display:

greenish hues subtly turning to crimson, then to endless shades of bronze.

The birds greet potential mates by gaping, exposing a bright indigo-blue mouth lining in stark contrast with the orange-yellow skin that covers both their face and throat. And while the male's deep, guttural grunts may terrify its rivals, they're music to the ears of those beauties awaiting Prince Charming. And what eyes: brilliant turquoise, rimmed with delicate dark-blue or green beads. Both sexes use their eyes to scan their territory for potential companions and, moments later, flirt with one.

Apparently smitten, the female approaches her suitor just as he throws his head back all the way to his rump, grunting noisily. Bill agape, revealing the striking blue lining, he lets his wings flop. The female quickly follows suit, catching the tiny branch her lover proffers. Copulation ensues, followed by mutual grooming. Newly formed couples shamelessly mimic each other and make booming declarations of love.

The male brings the material for the nest, and the female builds the nest. Then they live as a couple, and usually they both care for the young.

A Chinese fisherman accompanied by his two cormorant divers.

A cormorant fishing bird rests between dives.

Double-crested cormorants have striking turquoise eyes, rimmed with delicate dark-blue or green beads, and two rarely visible crests atop its head.

A cormorant dives for a fish.

Double-crested cormorants greet potential mates by gaping, exposing a bright indigo-blue mouth lining in stark contrast with the orange-yellow skin that covers their face and throat.

During courtship, the cormorant's black plumage takes on subtle blue, green, crimson, or bronze undertones.

A male cormorant makes a booming declaration of love.

A trio of grand
cormorants take
wing from a treetop
in China.

A cormorant lands on
a misty pond.

 COMMON RAVENS

A lone raven soars through a moody sky, perhaps looking for love.

Associated throughout history with mischief, villainy, and ill omens, the furtive and gravel-throated raven has long captured the imagination of people the world over. Edgar Allan Poe immortalized the bird in his famous poem, and scores of studies attest to its high degree of intelligence, surpassing, in some eyes, that of human beings.

The common raven—*Corvus corax*—is a large bird, 2 to 3 lbs (1 to 1.4 kg) and 24 to 27 inches long (60 to 70 cm) at maturity, with a wingspan of 48 to 52 inches (1.2 to 1.3 m). But let's not confuse it with the more common *Corvus corone*, or carrion crow, which is roughly half the size and lacks the raven's long, shaggy throat feathers.

Common ravens favor wooded areas and coastal regions, where they typically nest on sea cliffs or rocky escarpments. But it was on a high plateau in the Rocky Mountains of Banff that my wife and I chanced upon a duo in the midst of courtship—a rare sight.

It was an exceptionally sunny spring day, and the ravens' glossy black plumage gleamed in the radiant sun. The lovers were inseparable, grooming each other with their massive black bills—a perfect match for their plump silhouettes—and spreading their signature, wedge-shaped tails.

Like human teenagers, young ravens band together to play and—surprise, surprise—go out dating. They spend their time flying, catching objects on the wing, socializing, even fighting off larger predators. Which, come to think of it, is how human teenagers behave too. To court a female, the male puffs himself up and makes a series of bowing motions, his wings hanging limply and his tail spreading to display his iridescent plumage in the sunlight. Or he may perch on a tree branch, head inclined, seeking favors from his intended lover. At other times, he takes flight, reveling in spectacular acrobatics and urging her to join in. If the female obliges, they will soar and glide together, their dives and rolls growing increasingly complicated—the young lovers' way of getting acquainted. Their raucous croaking is unattractive at best, although in tender moments, the male instinctively knows how to modulate his voice, giving it a come-hither tone that his mate will respond to.

New couples form in winter or spring and will stay together for life—an unusual feat when you consider their lifespan: some individuals live well into their sixties and beyond, even reaching the centenary mark, according to the latest data. Solitary and less than sociable, ravens don't take kindly to humans. As I clicked away with my camera, for instance, our courting duo adopted the exasperated expression reminiscent of media celebrities trying to avoid the headlines.

Ravens often alternate between the two or three different nests that they build dizzyingly high up—on an overhanging cliff ledge, a treetop, or in tree cavities. It is made of twigs and sticks, and rimmed with moss and bark. Prior to egg laying, male and female chip in to renovate their nest, which can reach 48 inches thick (1.2 m), and 24 to 26 inches in diameter (60 to 70 cm).

Persecuted, much maligned, lumped together with their winter-time companions—wolves, foxes, and weasels—the ravens, those unpopular, astute, and wily characters of lore and legend, had at last granted us a peek inside their secret world, where playfulness and tenderness are the order of the day.

CHARACTERISTICS

Common raven (*Corvus corax*): Black with metallic glints; larger than the crow, with a thicker and more curved beak; shaggy throat feathers. **Distribution**: Canada, Alaska, Greenland, western United States and Mexico, Eurasia, and northern Africa

Normally secretive and solitary, a pair of courting common ravens is a rare sight. New couples form in winter or spring and will stay together for life.

Although both the common raven and carrion crow are black, the raven is nearly twice as big. The raven also has shaggy black neck feathers and a thicker beak.

A common raven perches on a well-worn sign in the Rocky Mountains.

RED-WINGED BLACKBIRDS

It's a truth universally acknowledged that the way we look or dress reflects an instinctive desire to stand out in a crowd, to attract those whom we find appealing while keeping others at arm's length. The same attitudes, as many studies have demonstrated, apply to male red-winged blackbirds, who readily flaunt their bright red, yellow-edged military-style epaulets—both to keep intruding males at bay and to attract female companions.

Every spring, these feathered sergeant majors return en masse from their wintering grounds throughout North America. From California to Florida and across Canada, we've seen and heard them by lost country roadsides and along crowded highways edged with dense vegetation. In city parks, cultivated fields, and isolated cattail and bulrush marshes we can't miss them. In the mating season they are everywhere—busy, noisy, and showing off.

Arriving early (mid-March or early April) in their reproduction quarters, the males are ready for action, and fights erupt almost instantaneously as the birds stake out their territory. They size up one another, then point their bills upward, spreading their wings and tails, highlighting the bright red epaulet feathers. A few seconds elapse before one of them—for reasons we humans don't fully appreciate—discreetly lowers his shoulders and retracts his head, covering the epaulets with its black plumage, apparently admitting defeat. With a flick of the feathers, as it were, aggressors are transformed into outcasts.

This kind of diplomatic jousting goes on at a noisy clip for three weeks, after which the losers beat a retreat and take up quarters in less desirable real estate. There they perch on tall grasses or picket fences, lining up in close formation, waiting for something to happen and resigned to their unfair lot in life.

Meanwhile, the female red wings are getting ready to migrate northward, in time for the conquerors' victory parade. They turn up sans epaulets, though still eminently eye-catching in their own modest way: brownish black plumage streaked with red, buff, or gray; buff eyebrows; buff median head stripe, shoulders, and throat, sometimes tinged with red or orange. Their understated livery, incidentally, blends nicely into nature, helping to shield their nestlings from hungry predators lurking in the swamps.

There are so many of them that they have to jostle for a place in the harem. A few cunning Don Juans, driven perhaps by unbridled libido or else a desire to have it all, go so far as to build fake nests in the hope of enticing even more females. The latter happily fall for the ruse, only to end up berating the sly, polygamous rascals for their deception.

But the ladies keep on coming, supplanting the previous wave who are now busy with mundane family duties—nest-building, egg-laying, incubating

---

CHARACTERISTICS

Red-winged blackbird (*Agelaius phoeniceus*): 7 to 9^1/$_2$ inches (18 to 24 cm). Male: glossy black feathers; red shoulder patches edged with buff or yellow. Female: brown on top, heavily streaked underparts; sometimes pinkish traces behind the eye. **Distribution**: North America except the far north, Mexico, Central America

---

Facing page: Red-wings are one of North America's most abundant bird species, and in the spring mating season male red-wings seem to be everywhere—busy, noisy, and showing off.

and feeding the young. Energized, the master grows increasingly vigilant, swiftly dispatching potential rivals and intruders who may be hanging around his domain. His sharp, pointy bill spares no one, least of all hapless birders such as me, who remained blissfully unaware of the *tchuck tchuck* warning calls, then paid the price in the form of painful lacerations to my unprotected head. (I learned my lesson!)

As summer fades to fall, the red wings—one of North America's most abundant bird species—disappear without warning. "Bye bye, blackbird" in the words of the old song. The resulting silent void is as poignant as it is short-lived. The normally raucous birds have simply retired within the confines of their remotest lairs in order to molt.

This autumnal rite strips them all of their carefully nurtured identities, not least those brilliant epaulets that lent the males such confidence and superiority. And so the little sergeant majors can only dream of the day when their sparkling feathers will return. Humans, too, share the same sartorial ambitions. As the sage long ago said, "Clothes maketh the man."

Male red-winged blackbirds flaunt their bright red, yellow-edged military-style epaulets to keep intruding males at bay and to attract females.

While the livery of male red-wings is designed to help them stand out, the female's helps them blend in. In the surrounding cattails, rushes, and grasses of her marshy habitat, her tawny hues and brown stripes are the perfect camouflage.

A red-wing blackbird nest lies carefully concealed among the rushes.

WHITE TERNS

The same long, sharp black beak that enables a white tern to mercilessly spear its lunch from the sea can also deliver a gentle caress to a mate.

Gently rocked by trade winds, our palm trees—rather curiously—sounded as if they were cooing. Denise and I looked at each other, at first puzzled, then incredulous, as we both recognized the distinctive voices of white terns. Sure enough, high up a giant palm, a pair were courting, doubtless exchanging vows of ever-lasting fidelity.

They were our surprise visitors that first holiday morning on a remote atoll of Polynesia—elegant tropical terns brilliantly and immaculately feathered, with long, thin bladelike bills that typically crested the waves with deadly effect. No careless creature—least of all, calamari—escapes the white tern's huge black eyes that, from dawn to dusk, scan the infinite sea for prey. At other times, the sharp bill is equally generous with caresses and tender stroking.

There are a few white tern refuges scattered about the world's three great oceans, places that are known only to those die-hard enthusiasts who are prepared to reward themselves with a few moments of ecstasy.

To see and photograph the "fairy terns" has long been a secret desire of mine. Our *faré*, a cozy, special Polynesian cabin built on the clear waters of the Pacific Ocean, is a good place from which to observe them. The white sand beach, the colorful fish we can see through the transparent waters below the faré, and the bright blue Pacific that seems without ends all contribute to the perfect setting for experiencing the love affair of the white terns.

The tern's large head gives it a stocky appearance, although you hardly notice it as the bird takes flight, fluid and elegant. Against the sunlight, its large and rounded wings become translucent, conferring an aura of mystery on these curious and seemingly sweet creatures.

Their exquisite beauty belies an existence governed by hard work. What's more—and this is an uncharacteristic feature—white terns waste neither time nor energy building nests. A slight recess, ideally located at an intersection between three strong, tall branches, is usually all it takes, although a few specimens prefer a rocky ridge or some elevated, nearly inaccessible spots. There, the female lays a single egg. To prevent their only offspring from falling, both the male and female terns restrain their own movements, taking turns incubating their young every two or three days. The "changing of the guard" takes place amid special precautions and an eccentric display of affection.

You can't mistake this paragon of a bird with its fine, steel blue feet for any other avian creature. Adulated by the first occupants of these idyllic islands, white terns eventually forgot that the world was a place full of danger. But everything changed with the arrival of European seafarers in search of a lost paradise. They'd barely reached the havens of these celestial fairies before they imposed their own wills on them, clearing land and forests to facilitate hunting and populating the meadows with calves, cows, sheep, and other farm animals. White terns made delicious eating, the settlers discovered, and the terns' eggs were a great delicacy.

CHARACTERISTICS

White tern (*Gygis alba*): Pristinely white; oversize head; disproportionately large black eyes; bill is long, thin, and black with bluish glints; steel blue feet. **Distribution**: Rare; tropical islands of the Pacific, Atlantic, and Indian oceans

The birds' plight worsened as fat mice eventually made their appearance, inevitably accompanied by the mice's eternal enemies—cats. The slaughter was awesome. Today, specialists try to gauge the damage done to the tern population by counting the birds' bones in the ashes of kitchen fires; they are finding legion.

In danger of extinction, these symbols of love and wondrousness take refuge in far-flung, isolated spots, attracting the attention of only a precious few. But then a couple and their young happened by my 800-millimeter lens, as if pleading for their right to live, to love. I promised myself to make their plight understood.

In danger of extinction, white terns now live in far-flung, isolated tropical islands, attracting the attention of only a precious few. White terns have large white heads and disproportionately huge black eyes.

A white tern takes wing, the sun glowing behind its fine tip feathers.

ROYAL TERNS

Royal terns live and breed in large, crowded colonies.

At the last moment the sputtering, wheezing motor of our Zodiac comes to a complete stop, letting the rising tide propel us gently toward the solitary, picture-postcard island off the coast of southern Texas. Our friend and guide from San Antonio had promised us a staggering sight, and we are amazed and captivated. From our small boat we can see royal terns milling about the sandy beach, their identity betrayed by their black caps and long, sharp, orange bills. Even though our approach is silent, some are disturbed and begin squawking stridently.

The cacophony grows louder by the minute, climaxing in a deafening clamor. Tens, then hundreds of birds hurl themselves into the air. Several seize the opportunity to fly farther out, where we can see them swooping down into the water then rising again with silvery, wriggling loot clasped in their bills. The flight back to shore is anything but tranquil. Kleptoparasites appear out of nowhere, furiously pursuing the hapless fish catchers, harassing them into dropping their prey, then catching it on the wing. This happens over and over again, and the resulting racket is terrific.

Meanwhile, those birds closer to shore seem serene to a fault, utterly oblivious to the drama unfolding over the open sea. Couples twirl in tandem, soaring and diving with abandon before gliding to a smooth landing on the white sand.

One pair in particular catches our attention. As we watch, the male pirouettes exuberantly, engaging his heart's desire in a so-called fish flight, billing and cooing before tendering his precious catch. At first she hesitates, then, taking a closer look at the offering, tastes it before gazing admiringly at her suitor. We all know what happens next. Lucky bird!

Nearby, another couple doesn't fare as well. The female is half-heartedly picking at her food with the tip of her bill—always a bad sign. Still, what's unappealing to one tern's taste buds may be delectable to another, and greedy onlookers are never far away, keeping a beady eye on fussing couples in the hope of stealing a savory dessert while no one's paying attention.

Some females, we're told, are cunning and expect a constant supply of edible sea delicacies. Lazy or recalcitrant caterers will be summarily dismissed.

When it comes to the business of mating, female terns call the shots. A suitor, whether a Don Juan or neophyte, must first gain the astute lady's confidence. She carefully scrutinizes the candidates as they plunge like dive-bombers to catch fish, or steal food from one another and from other seabirds. Then she chooses the best and boldest individual and joins him in the courtship flight. The black, spiky crest is definitely an asset. It's believed to be a powerful turn-on for the ladies, as well as a handy weapon to keep rivals and other intruders at bay.

Nest-building skills, on the other hand, are not a prerequisite. Royal terns live in casually dug depressions on a sandy beach or marshy lagoon, using the sun's rays to keep warm. They prefer nesting in large, crowded colonies on isolated islands that are off limits to raccoons or other pred-

CHARACTERISTICS
Royal tern (*Sterna maxima*): Second-largest species of tern, 16 to 18 inches (40 to 46 cm) long, with a wingspan between 37 to 39 inches (92 to 97 cm); shaggy black crown feathers; large orangish tapered bill; forked tail. **Distribution**: East, west, and gulf coasts of the United States, Mexico, Central America, South America, West Indies, western Africa

ators. They favor flat, sandy terrain that is ceaselessly remodeled by wind and tide, and they willingly share the area with other tern species.

But survival means learning to fend for oneself early on in life, and the lessons are endless. The birds learn to hover some 33 to 66 feet (10 to 20 m) above sea level, spot fish and other prey in the water, then dive and use their wings to swim and catch the food. And that's not all. The birds must also master the tricky business of hanging on to the wriggling fish, the hard-shelled crayfish, or the slippery mollusk. They also learn to regurgitate their partially digested meals for their young without suffocating. And so it goes from one generation to another—there is simply no letup.

We arrived in silence, and now we are leaving this beautiful wild reserve with a silent wish: may this secluded bird paradise last forever!

The fluffy young royal tern on the left will eventually resemble the sleek adult male, with a spiky black crest and long orange beak.

Royals are the second-largest tern species and have wingspans of more than three feet.

A female royal tern tastes the offering brought by her suitor, while greedy onlookers wait for a chance to steal a morsel when the couple is distracted.

A male royal tern brings another wriggling, fishy gift for his lady.

MUTE SWANS

This year my brother, who lives in Vancouver, invited the whole family for a spring vacation. Happily, the children, Denise, and I accepted the invitation, although we also had an ulterior motive: do a little birding in the West.

Many lakes and parks adorn this region, and they abound with birds. One afternoon, we were walking around a beautiful lake in search of something unusual, and we came to a big nest right on the bank. Seeing no birds, we wondered what species could use such a big nest. Lifting our eyes toward the water, we saw the answer—and an unforgettable spectacle. Swans in love!

Boasting long, elegant S-shaped necks and clad in as many as 25,000 pristinely white feathers, mute swans (*Cygnus olor*) are instantly recognizable. They are one of the three swan species found in North America. The other two are the trumpet swans (*Cygnus buccinator*) and the whistling or tundra swans (*Cygnus columbianus*). All three derive their names from the sound and character of their calls. The mutes are generally quiet, but hardly mute—they hiss, grunt, and, whenever they feel threatened, snort. Nowadays they can be found both in the wild and in manmade habitats, gracing ponds, lakes, and wetlands.

Couples stay together for a very long time, if not quite for life, "renewing their vows" every spring. Nonbreeding males, including immature birds, tend to congregate in flocks until they are ready to engage one another in bloody skirmishes over territory, food, and unattached females.

The mutes will occasionally pair up when they are as young as two years old, practicing abstinence until they mature, usually at three. If there happens to be a housing crisis, breeding-age birds will remain celibate while they roam through tall aquatic grasses in search of an abode.

But if nesting territory is plentiful, a duo will happily stake out a home to call their own even before they are old enough to breed. Vigorously repelling intruders, they celebrate their triumphant defenses by rising majestically on their feet and loudly flapping their powerful wings. They also engage in courtship rituals. First the male, or cob, shakes its head from right to left in order to ruffle up its neck feathers. The fiancée, or pen, follows suit to signal her consent. They lean forward, wings and necks outstretched, embracing each other, hissing sweetly. Soon after, the cob mounts his lover before they both dip their heads into the water. Most couples copulate frequently, even after all the eggs have been laid for the coming season.

Watching our pair on the lake dance and caress each other was quite a thrill. After their copulation, the female preened and washed herself for a long moment before she came back to her nest, followed by her eager mate. They were too busy to even notice us, and we moved off silently, convinced that we had seen a magic moment.

CHARACTERISTICS

Mute swan (*Cygnus olor*): Graceful silhouette; pristinely white feathers; orange bill, black protuberance at the base. **Distribution**: Dispersed irregularly over Eurasia; introduced in North America, South Africa, Australia, and New Zealand

Facing page:
A cob and pen mute swan pair nuzzle each other.

A pair of mute swan lovers tends their secluded lakeshore nest. Couples stay together for a very long time, if not quite for life, renewing their vows each spring.

With its long, graceful neck and head, and its distinctive orange bill with black base, the mute swan is instantly recognizable.

THE MYTHICAL SWAN

Swans have captured the popular imagination for centuries, featured prominently in Greek mythology and fairy tales as potent symbols of tumultuous love, rivalries, strength, power, and nobility. According to one Greek legend, Zeus, supreme deity of the celestial realm, son of Kronos and Rhea, transformed himself into a beautiful swan in order to seduce the Spartan queen, Leda. Another legend involves Apollo, the Greek god of music, poetry, prophecy, and medicine, who journeyed to the land of the eternal sun, driving a chariot pulled by swans.

And who can easily forget the poignant fable that recounts the story of the mute swan that starts to sing as death approaches? This is the legend that gave the English language a familiar phrase—"swan song"—referring to a work or performance created toward the end of an artist's career.

From ancient mythology to our modern times, the swan is still a symbol of grace, nobility, and honor. As the well-known tale from Hans Christian Andersen, "The Ugly Duckling," says: "To be born in a duck's nest, in a farmyard, is of no consequence to a bird, if it is hatched from a swan's egg."

A mute swan dances on the surface of the water, spreading its wings to ward off intruders.

Mute swan parents take the cygnets out for a family swim.

The cob and pen (male and female mute swans) lovingly rub heads on the water.

$\mathcal{R}$ED-HEADED WEAVERS

The red-headed weaver is one of more than a hundred weaver species, so named because the males built intricate nests to attract their mates.

CHARACTERISTICS

Red-headed weaver (*Anaplectes rubriceps*): 5 1/2 to 6 inches (14 to 15 cm). Male: head, upper breast, and mantle are bright red; white lower breast; black face mask. Female: brownish body; bill, wing, and tail tips are orangish red. **Distribution**: Central to south Africa

My wife and I were traveling in Kenya with two members of the Kikuyu tribe, one serving as our guide and the other as our cook and camping organizer. We had to purchase our food, mainly live fish and chickens, from the villagers in the area we were traveling through. One day, while our guides were shopping for our next meal, we strolled along a cliff, hoping to see birds of prey. But what appeared was a beautiful red-headed weaver.

As we watched, bewildered, the little chap gathered material and started to build a nest. He seemed to have a rough time with these dry twigs. Usually weavers use fresh grass stems, but they were unavailable here in this arid region. He was only at the initial stage—building the ring around which the rest of his nest would take form—but his frenzy was such a delightful sight. As we learned later, this nest was designed to attract a mate.

The red-headed weaver is common in the region from Sénégal to Kenya and down to South Africa. It is one of 118 species in the family ploceidae (weavers in general), which owe their names to the fact that the males use their nimble toes and strong, conical beaks to weave highly intricate hanging nests out of grass and palm leaves in order to attract females.

For most weaver species, including the red-headed, the male gets to work with the advent of the rainy season. First he picks a spot from which to hang his love nest—the farther out of reach of snakes, lizards, and even larger birds, the better. The tip of a thin, pliant tree branch or palm frond is a good bet.

Next, he takes advantage of prime construction material: green shoots and fresh rootlets, which are more flexible—and therefore more resilient—than hard, dry twigs. He uses these to build a kind of scaffolding between plant stems or a basket shape that hangs from a single twig. Comfortably and securely perched, he begins to weave. Using both his beak and feet, he tears strips of leaves and stems, tying them into knots, making interlocking loops, reversing the pattern from one row to the next, inserting fresh strips into the fabric as he goes along. Soon a ring—the entrance—has been formed around the bird, followed by a basket on the side—the nest chamber—and before you know it, construction is complete. The more experienced the builder, the sturdier and more tightly woven the nest. He may intertwine leaves at the top of the nest to make it more waterproof.

But it's the ever-fastidious female that puts the seal of approval on this piece of real estate. The fortunes of those proud male nest-builders depend solely on the whims of their prospective companions who, for the sake of a faulty weave or an eye-pleasing design, will either reject or embrace them. All too often, alas, love hangs by a single thread. If a female finds his work unsatisfactory and leaves, the suitor, ever the perfectionist, will then tear apart the entire structure and go back to the drawing board, hoping for better luck with the next female. Interestingly enough, some clever and cautious males actually tie their knots a tad loosely, as if anticipating failure, in which case they can undo the construction more easily.

On the other hand, if Madame likes what she sees, then she'll mate with the builder and promptly move in. She'll give the residence a few finishing touches, lining it with grass and other soft materials, making it fit for laying eggs and raising her chicks—"but all by myself, if you don't mind."

In either case, the lover gets the old heave-ho, fated to continue building more nests.

A weaver may build his nest between a pair of branches or, like this one, suspended like a hanging basket from a single branch.

THE CAPE WEAVER

Weavers are generally monogamous, but some species, like the cape weaver, prefer a harem. Male cape weavers may have as many as seven brides. Once a female accepts his nest and settles in, he usually builds another in the immediate vicinity, such as on neighboring branches.

Cape weavers are $6^1/2$ to 7 (17 to 18 cm) tall. They have yellow heads and underparts, and their upper parts are olive green and streaked with olive brown. Their yellow face is more or less washed with chestnut brown. These polygamous weavers are very territorial.

I photographed this busy male cape weaver on a trip to South Africa, where it is endemic.

WHITE IBISES

A pair of white ibises rub up against each other.

Through the narrow openings of our blind, Denise and I glimpse a flock of gregarious birds flying in a V formation in the distance. As they approach, we spot a string of male white ibises in their midst, conspicuous by their down-curved red bills, outstretched necks, and long, bright red legs. These birds are arguably one of the most spectacular species to grace the North American sky. Moments later they alight, resting and preening at the edge of the lake before us, grunting loudly, ready to stake out their nesting territory here in the Florida Everglades.

Predictably, the females show up a few days later. They are easily identified by their smaller size and shorter bills. They perch on tree branches and nonchalantly eye the loquacious males, checking out their future partners. From time to time, one of them gingerly advances to proffer her beak to a particular gent—only to be rudely rebuffed! The furious male, mistaking her well-meaning gesture for an act of territorial aggression, responds in kind. He brandishes his fiery red bill like a sword, missing the hastily retreating female by a feather, as it were.

She should have known better. Love among the ibises means staying put and letting the male make the first move. And he invariably does. He strikes his potential mate with flapping wings and shakes her like a rag doll, showcasing his qualities as a strong, determined, and worthy patriarch.

Courtship rituals of a more romantic bent come later, in the form of complex aerial displays, followed by playful jousting or quieter periods on land. The lovers typically extend their necks forward, locking themselves in a tender embrace, preening each other, and rubbing their heads together. The ruffian of before has transformed himself into a charming prince, stroking his loved one with his bill, carefully smoothing and rearranging her feathers. Such behavior is repeated over and over across the vast colonies, and before you know it, the lovebirds have disappeared behind some handy bushes to consummate their passion.

Incidentally, while white ibises are socially monogamous, they can't resist the occasional fling—with a neighbor, for example—and readily engage in extrapair copulation.

Nest building is a cooperative effort. The female chooses the site—which can be in a tree, a bush or shrub, as long as it's near the water—and is personally responsible for the construction. Gathering materials—sticks and twigs—is the male's domain, and he often obtains them by raiding their neighbors' nests.

Young white ibises will molt several times before growing the white feathers that mark adulthood. Then they must fine-tune the complex, elegant mating habits that characterize their species and are crucial for their survival.

The birds' unique rituals, so bold and yet so seductive, are said to have inspired long-ago sorcerers to transform themselves into ibises and use their plumage to appease the angry gods. They believed that by looking like these magnificent birds they would acquire their beauty and their assurance.

CHARACTERISTICS

White ibis (*Eudocimus albus*): White when nesting; long red or orange curved bill; bare skin in eye area; red or orangish feet. **Distribution**: Southern United States to Venezuela

This is a relatively small group of white ibises; they normally live in vast colonies.

White ibises are easily identified by their scimitar-like bills and long, fiery red legs.

A flock of ibises fly before the moon.

SCARLET IBISES AND PINK HYBRIDS

The ibis family, *Threskiornithidae*, is made up of 33 species, including the scarlet ibis, which breeds in Central and South America. The bird is said to derive its red plumage from its diet of carotene-rich crustaceans, shrimps being a favorite treat.

The scarlet ibises' presence in North America may have originated in 1961, when scientists placed twenty-four scarlet ibis eggs in the nests of white ibises in southern Florida. Seventeen hatched and went on to crossbreed with their white cousins, producing what are commonly known as hybrid ibises, with faded pink feathers. These pink hybrids are relatively rare. (For example, there are only couples listed in Venezuela.)

There is much debate about whether white and scarlet ibises are actually members of the same species, differing only in color. At the moment, they have distinct scientific names, while the hybrids do not.

The scarlet ibis is said to derive its color from its diet of carotene-rich crustaceans, such as shrimp.

A rare, pink hybrid ibis is the result of coupling between a white and a scarlet ibis.

A white ibis patrols the surf.

Left: An ibis couple watch the sun set together.

DEMOISELLE CRANES

Demoiselle cranes have the slender, graceful neck typical of all cranes, but the ear-level tufts of feathers are unique to the species.

For many experienced birders, cranes, with their remarkably robust physiques, have no equals.

In 1996 we were enjoying an adventurous trip in India with a few friends. We had just spent two fascinating days in beautiful Jodhpur, "the blue city," and were moving on to the well-known Bharatpur Keoladeo wild-bird paradise to see the famous endangered Siberian crane. But on the way there, we had an unexpected encounter with a crane of another kind.

Driving through very green and luxurious countryside, we came to a small marsh lake, where stood hundreds of demoiselle cranes. The spectacular birds, the smallest but not the least of the cranes, were exuberant, jumping and emitting low-pitched and raspy calls. They were not exactly mating, but rather reinforcing their relationships.

Like all crane species, demoiselles are endowed with flexible and slender bodies. And, like all crane species, they seem to dance at every opportunity and for a variety of reasons: to attract mates, reinforce pair bonds, keep intruders at bay, and even just for the sheer pleasure of it. Young adult birds breed dance for hours on end. They dance as if in a trance, always fine-tuning their increasingly complex choreography. The older, more experienced birds, on the other hand, merely go through the motions. Already paired, they are more anxious to get straight to the conjugal act itself, considering such displays as little more than unavoidable, albeit intense, preliminary steps leading up to the ultimate pleasure.

Demoiselle cranes follow the traditional crane courtship ritual. The male and female stand side by side, raising their heads and necks in unison and uttering soft, purring calls. Then they break into a chase, their sail-like wings unfurling and flapping. The routine accelerates to include bowing, prancing, and leaping into the air. It's easy to tell when the male is aroused, for he flaps his ruffled feathers loudly—to the apparent delight of his beloved. From time to time, one partner or the other picks up a small branch or twig off the ground and tosses it into the air, all the while emitting a series of calls. All of these coordinated actions reinforce the already strong bond that unites them until death.

At last the inevitable moment comes, and the breathless female pauses to part her wings, unequivocally signaling that she's ready. The patient companion promptly mounts her back, vigorously shaking his plumage for balance and stability. During the act, they preen each other with their bills, bodies quivering. Then the precariously balanced male hops back down onto firm ground, and it is all over. It was a fleeting moment, lasting only a few seconds, but nonetheless crucial for the survival of the species.

Soon they resume the energetic dance, and before long, the euphoria spreads contagiously through the entire flock, climaxing in a wild sexual delirium. Mute and languorous calls accompany the increasingly lascivious, intoxicating movements.

CHARACTERISTICS
Demoiselle crane (*Grus virgo*): Sexes look alike; small; gray; head, front of neck, and chest black; only crane whose head is entirely feathered, with distinctive white tufts at ear level. **Distribution**: India, central Eurasia

Then the fever subsides and the need for self-expression wanes, only to suddenly begin again as a way of releasing tension and anxiety. Instead of tiring out the birds, the frantic activity seems to produce a relaxing effect, so much so that copulation proves to be highly successful. Each male eagerly invents ever more intricate and novel dance steps to attract his beloved partner. She quickly responds with great leaping bounds, prancing round and round her feverish companion. This in turn excites and encourages the younger cranes to follow suit. For immature birds, these spectacles are little more than an excuse for competition and muscle training; sometimes they help the males work off their aggression or, more frequently, fine-tune their gestures and attitudes. Even day-old chicks show a natural talent for this avian disco.

Sooner or later, of course, couples will feel a compelling need to build a house and home. Their collective energies will then be transferred to their offspring, teaching them to imitate the dazzling dance steps and powerful wingbeats that characterize their ballets of desire.

At the beginning of the traditional crane courtship dance, the male and female stand side by side, raising their heads and necks in unison and uttering soft, purring calls.

A pair of demoiselles wades through the water.

Demoiselle cranes congregate on a small lake in India.

THE WORLD'S ENDANGERED CRANES

Denise and I have come across our share of these various species of elegant, long-legged wading birds, whose extraordinary enthusiasm for dancing has made our encounters with them memorable. But often, as I have watched them through the early morning mists, I seemed to sense a note of anxiety mixed into the birds' great, hoarse calls.

Cranes are among the planet's most threatened birds. Out of the fifteen species that make up the family *Gruidae*, a whopping eleven are thought to be in danger of extinction. There are two subfamilies. The *Balearicinae*, or crowned-crane subfamily, has two species: the black-crowned and the gray-crowned. Breeding exclusively in Africa, these two species roost in trees and cannot abide extreme cold.

The *Gruinae* subfamily, or typical cranes, can be found all over the world except Antarctica and South America. This subfamily consists of the remaining 13 species: the black-necked, blue, brolga, common, demoiselle, hooded, red-crowned (or Japanese), sandhill, sarus, Siberian, wattled, white-naped, and whooping. These species are hardier than their crowned cousins and prefer nesting on the ground—in shallow marshes, for example. Also, their calls are louder. The sandhill crane can be seen in the United States and Canada.

The Siberian crane (*Grus leucogeranus*) is especially rare; there are only a few thousand left in the entire world, and the species is in great danger of extinction. As its name implies, these birds spend summers in Siberia, and they winter in China and in India's Keoladeo Bhartpur Park. It was in India in 1996 that I took pictures of a trio of migrating Siberian cranes. There were only three, and it was the first time in years that they had come back to India. Their appearance was mentioned in the newspaper and on TV. You can see that they are banded, probably by the curators of the Keoladeo park. The International Crane Foundation reports that Siberian cranes have not been in India since 2002.

Denise and I got to add a new crane on our birders' checklist in autumn 2005 on a trip to South Africa. The rare, exquisite blue crane is the most range restricted of the cranes. It can be seen mainly in the Cape region of South Africa. After a 300-mile drive from Cape Town, on a cloudy and foggy day, we had the chance to observe a small flock of blue cranes, grazing in planted fields. We had dreamed of seeing those "paradise cranes," and it was a treat to observe them moving around so elegantly and communicating with each other by sound and postures. Every moment we watched was worth the long trip.

Humans continue to encroach on the cranes' habitats all over the world, and in some areas, people kill the birds because they perceive them as crop-eating enemies. I often wonder if in the future these magnificent birds will have enough living room to pursue their prodigious dance steps away from prying eyes, and to continue those activities that may seem frivolous, but which, at the most basic level, are central to their existence.

The brolga crane (*Grus rubicunda*) of Australia is very large. It is predominantly gray and has red patches on its head; its feet are black.

Endemic to South Africa, the rare, small blue crane (*Anthropoides paradiseus*) is ashy gray with a white forehead. Its large wings have black elongated primary, secondary, and teritary feathers that reach to the ground.

The rare Siberian crane (*Grus leucogeranus*) is near extinction. It has white plumage, and its face and feet are red.

The common crane (*Grus grus*) lives mainly in Eurasia, but spends its winters in India and Africa. Large and predominantly gray, the bird has a small red patch on top of its head, and its forehead is black. The front of its neck is also black, while the back of its neck is white.

A native of Uganda, Kenya, Zimbabwe, and Mozambique, the gray-crowned crane (*Balearica regulorum*) is more colorful than other cranes. Despite its name, its crown is actually golden in color.

North America's own sandhill crane (*Grus canadensis*) resembles a heron.
Like the heron, it is tall and flies with its neck and feet outstretched. Its slate
coloring is often tinged with rust, and it has a red forehead.

Common Loons

Come spring, loons shed their gray winter plumage in favor of their wedding attire: a classy black and white back, glossy black head, and white-barred collar.

CHARACTERISTICS

Common loon (*Gavia immer*): Male and female are identical; large head and neck black with greenish or pinkish accents; white-barred collar, straight slender black bill; black and white checkered back; white abdomen. **Distribution**: Northern North America, Greenland, and Iceland; winters along the coasts of the United States and northwest Europe

In the heart of a secluded lake, in Quebec's La Vérendrye Wildlife Reserve, the silence is almost palpable. Moments later it is broken by a peal of eerie cries not unlike the voice of a Tyrolian mountaineer. The tenant of this watery domain has unmistakably announced his return to home base. For generations, right after the ice melts, the male bird has sent forth his heart-tugging appeals. He's unhappy all by himself and wants a companion. Somewhere beyond the mist covering the surface of the lake an echo answers the call, followed by a veritable cascade of haunting notes, prolonged and insistent. The pair of common loons have found each other. I feel a special thrill.

Almost imperceptibly, the plaintive calls float closer. Then, less than 100 feet (30 m) away, a pair of phantoms with bulky skulls and straight, tapering bills emerge from the gloom. I propel the canoe smoothly over the surface of the water, the way my old Algonquin guide taught me many moons ago. I had met this fascinating man when I was a college boy, on a canoe and camping trip up north, and I will always remember his knowledge and respect for nature. With a ventriloquist's skill, that tireless paddler shared his fascination for the common loon with me.

At the first sign of spring, the loon's drab gray winter plumage is gradually replaced, feather by feather, by nuptial splendor. Shades of glossy black, accented with shimmering greens and pinks, cap his head, and a white-barred collar adorns his throat. His back is checkered with black and white, in stark contrast with his white breast and belly, which, when he's aroused, rise proudly above the water.

The new couple will eventually establish a more resilient partnership than those formed by Pacific loons or their cousins, the red-throated loons. The common loons exchange languorous, flutelike notes. Moments later, swathed in a heavy mist, the male resumes his plaintive call; it both charms and sends shivers down the spine, rather like the howl of a wolf. Aiming my camera, I click away, all too aware, alas, that I can never fully capture the magic of the moment.

Gaining confidence, the male turns up the volume, while the object of his attention feigns indifference and moves farther away. After putting some distance between them, however, she turns around, suddenly all coyness and complacency. The lovers greet each other, then proceed to dive and pirouette. Like members of a synchronized swimming team, they break through the surface in unison. Completely absorbed, the birds forget all about me, multiplying their arabesques, raising and lowering their long beaks in sharp staccato movements so that at times they intersect. They have a habit of submerging their rear ends so that their chest feathers and shoulders are clearly displayed, before they stretch out their necks as far as possible.

Each bird then takes off in an opposite direction, cutting a wide circle through the water and

With haunting calls, a lone loon will announce his arrival at his summer home and beckon longingly to his mate.

ultimately coming back to the starting point. Wild, throaty laughter stimulates their passion. At the height of their excitement, they stand up on their tails, strenuously beating their wings in order to display their white breasts provocatively. Sometimes, as my Algonquin guide used to note, a lonely or jealous bachelor—or even a couple of beginners anxious to learn about the facts of life—intervene, join in the ball and execute a few new steps before disappearing as unexpectedly as they turned up.

At last, the belle steps onto the shore and assumes the much-anticipated posture—lying flat, neck flush to the ground—that no companion can possibly ignore. From that moment, nothing will stop them. The bouts of lovemaking are so intense that a slight depression, known as a false nest, appears in the moist humus.

Clumsy and awkward on dry land, the pair rarely venture there, always taking care to set up their nest, a mound of decomposing vegetation, near the water. They often choose a sloping muskrat den or install themselves near an island far removed from predators.

United for life, male and female—their plumage indistinguishable—frequent freshwater rivers or an uninhabited lake, territory that they refuse to share with their own kind if it happens to be less than 2.5 acres (5 ha) in area.

Finally, one misty morning toward the end of the season, the sound of a long, syncopated lament, filtering through the milky mists rising from the water, comes for the last time. Then it fades, like an echo of romance. And once again, silence envelops the lake.

Proud parents take their young offspring for a swim.

United for life, a loon couple usually will not share their waters with others of their kind.

A loon flaps its wings to dry them in the morning sunlight.

CEDAR WAXWINGS

Cherry blossoms and cedar waxwings herald the arrival of spring in North America.

CHARACTERISTICS
Cedar waxwing (*Bombycilla cedrorum*): Velvety, clear brown plumage; yellowish chest; raised crest; black face mask. **Distribution**: All of North America, except the far north

The arrival of spring, with its new warmth, its abundance of flowers, and its sweet smells, is the ideal time to take a vacation. For my wife and me, a long weekend in Maine, with its charming small towns and blooming trees, was a perfect setting.

Very early one morning, we found a cozy little park. There was no one around but us two and dozens of busy cedar waxwings, singing and flying among the fragrant blossoms of the apple and cherry trees. It was a good picture of what heaven could be!

Half hidden by the spring-green tracery and silhouetted against the morning sun, the velvet-smooth vagabonds—their sleek plumage looks more like fur than feathers—plundered the sweet-tasting flower petals with abandon. Garbed in a tawny livery, tails tipped with a fluorescent yellow band, shading to orange at times, the hungry birds eagerly filled up on confetti-like blossoms.

But as we watched them in delight, I noticed that they were offering petals to each other. Sometimes one would eat the petal, sometimes one would refuse the present. I realized that we were witnessing the vows of a rather unconventional wedding ceremony.

Romance among waxwings usually begins during the birds' nomadic migrations. More often than not, the male starts out by executing a series of little sideways hopping movements that bring him close to his intended. Depending on the season and location, he brings her a petal, an insect, or a berry. She accepts the gift, then hops a short distance away, only to turn around and hand it back to the male, who quickly offers it to her again. The exercise resembles a miniature ballet driven by one bird's courtesy and the other's appetite. The players in this little exchange can keep it up for 15 or 20 minutes, at which point one or the other decides to gobble up the gift.

Perhaps because they are near-sighted, absent-minded, or ambivalent, some waxwings will sidle up to a member of their own sex, with predictable results. The offended bird will become irritated, even violent—beating its wings furiously, stretching out its neck, and thrusting its head toward the intruder.

Once the misunderstanding is resolved, peace and quiet return to the blossom-laden tree. The birds gorge themselves from their well-stocked pantry until they can eat no more, forgetting all about the time and simply postponing the business of hatching the next generation.

Construction of the conjugal nest does not begin until autumn. Then, making up for lost time, the cedar waxwings set to work with a vengeance, building a second nest while they're still busily engaged in looking after the first brood. Snowed under by the sheer volume of tasks, the male—as if emboldened by the anonymity provided by his carnival mask—helps himself to his neighbors' nesting materials.

No sooner is their work done than the indomitable "skirt chasers" answer the call of freedom and the open road and head for pastures new. While the females incubate the eggs, the males usually return to feed them. But sometimes the expectant fathers gather together by themselves for a little snack—a sort of avian boys' night out. Then one late autumn afternoon, when the fruits are bursting with ripeness, these finicky gourmands, both male and female, are back again. Feasting on small sugar-sweet berries and pilfering slightly fermented grapes, the birds become more than a little tipsy.

Strength restored, they begin their adventurous journey southward. In a few months, that journey will perhaps bring them back to the place where the cherry blossoms fall like snow.

Feasting on the overripe, slightly fermented berries of autumn can make cedar waxwings more than a little tipsy.

WHY ARE THEY CALLED WAXWINGS?

Cedar waxwings of both sexes—they are virtually indistinguishable—hop about from branch to branch, fluttering long wings tipped by red droplets. These adornments have what appears to be a waxy texture—in fact, it is more like plastic—which, according to some experts, can indicate age, social standing, and even "matrimonial" status. Others believe that they help protect the delicate feathers from wear and tear caused by the needles of the conifers where the birds tend to congregate and rest.

The early explorers of New France (North American territory claimed by the French in the eighteenth century) singled out this particular feature to give the bird its common name—waxwing. Struck by the bird's cinnamon tones and a hooded crest that resembles a missionary's habit, they informally christened it the *récollet*—or friar.

The wings of the cedar waxwing have red, plastic-like tips—hence their name. Only the birds know for sure which of them is male and female, as the sexes are identical in color and size.

OSTRICHES

Beauty is in the eye of the beholder, as this trio of ostriches prove.

In the heart of the Kenyan savanna a column of dust appeared out of nowhere, followed immediately by another. Approaching at rapid speed, the dust squalls multiplied. It took a little while before I could identify the ostriches amid the haze.

They were racing—or rather following—each other, speeding toward us in ten-foot (3-m) strides; muscular thighs powered their disproportionately long legs, which end in two toes with formidable claws. Each tiny, bald head sat on the end of an improbably long, periscope-like neck. Standing through the open roof of our Land Rover, we were almost eye to eye with them. Ostriches' eyes are huge, even bigger than those of the elephant. And those long, come-hither eyelashes are to die for!

These 8.5-foot giants can weigh more than 220 pounds (100 kg), but they always carry themselves with grace. Unable to fly, the ostrich carries rudimentary wings that seem to float uselessly at its sides. But by skillfully adjusting their positions, the bird can turn on a dime, quickly changing directions, even when moving at high speed.

These champions of the racing-bird communicate through their physical comportment and posturing. As we watched the group, each bird defiantly sized up the others. Generally highly sociable, members of *Struthio camelus* nevertheless divide into two groups during the mating season. With males on one side and females on the other, this is one period of the year when they put aside their strong clan spirit.

The male, dressed in his finest white and jet black, establishes the boundaries of his territory by letting loose with a sound reminiscent of—believe it or not—a lion's roar. Equally aggressive, his rivals battle him and one another and end up seriously scarred. The male ostrich has an impressive penis that can be up to 12 inches (30 cm) long.

During their display dance, the males beat their wings incessantly, raising and lowering them in a seductive effect that works magic on the female onlookers. Charmed by these displays of strength, elegance, and skill, the ladies, decked out in uniformly brown feathers—which serve as camouflage on the tawny savanna—come running.

It's now time for the females to make their preferences known. Each bird approaches her chosen one and, seemingly in a trance, urinates on the ground to imbue it with her odor. The capricious male haughtily feigns indifference, so the indefatigable female repeats the act. Having finally made up his mind, our hero pursues her, flapping his wings. At the same time the bare parts of his anatomy—his head, neck, and thighs—take on a red tint that is, apparently, irresistible. The female lowers her wings, her tail, and her head and, sitting down on the ground, invites her companion to consummate their courtship.

The reproductive frenzy takes hold of the other birds who witness this scene, and before you know it, "swapping" is in progress. A male may be polygamous and have a number of concubines. The latter,

CHARACTERISTICS

Ostrich (*Struthio camelus*): Small, bare head; large prominent eyes with long lashes; periscope-like neck; long robust feet with horny patches; two solid toes with claws. Male: Black and white plumage, partially bare during mating season; head and neck reddish. Female: Evenly brownish; head and neck grayish. **Distribution**: Africa

however, must obtain the consent of the main hen, or dominant female, to mate with him. Otherwise she will drive them away. The male and the main hen sometimes form a couple for many years, while the minor hens come and go.

After having serviced each member of his harem (usually three or four) the male selects the spot for the nest, a simple hole 3.5 feet (1 m) in diameter and 12 inches (30 cm) deep in the sand. Next, he lines the nest with soft feathers. The main hen starts the clutch and lays eggs every two days. She usually lays five to eight all together, but she can have as few as two and as many as eighteen. The other females then take turns depositing one or two eggs. The more the main hen likes her, the more eggs a minor female is allowed to add to the nest.

The largest in the world, each egg weighs in at around 3.5 pounds (1.5 kg) and is 6 inches (16 cm) in diameter. The main hen can incubate only 19 to 25 eggs. Recognizing her own eggs by their size, weight, or pore structure, she puts them in the middle of the nest and pushes the other ones around to cover them. When it comes to reproducing, the ostriches' theme seems to be "Why make it simple when one can make it complicated?"

After that, the dominant female chases off her rivals and begins the brooding process, tending the eggs from morning to evening, while her Casanova takes over the night shift.

The ostrich holds a record of superlatives in the avian world: it is the largest, tallest, and heaviest living bird; it has the biggest eggs; and, most impressive of all, it is the fastest runner—one that can outrun many mammals, including two birders in a Land Rover.

A trio of ostriches on the African plain.

An ostrich double date: two females and two males. The males are distinguishable by their pink heads, necks, and thighs and their white and jet black plumage.

When he's ready to mate, a male ostrich's face takes on a red tint.

The ostrich couple shares brooding duties. The female warms the nest during the day, while males, such as this one, usually take the night shift.

An ostrich takes a
beauty bath in the dust.

Mama and Papa Ostrich watch over their recently
hatched brood.

Young ostriches have rough, course plumage that
makes them look rather like hedgehogs.

An ostrich keeps proud watch over her brood.

The sun sets on another day of ostrich romance.

Northern Gannets

After lovemaking, a northern gannet couple cements their nuptial bond with some mutual preening.

CHARACTERISTICS

Northern gannet (*Morus bassanus*): Large white marine bird; back of head yellowish; wings and body tapered; black wingtips; blue-gray eyes rimmed with black or deep blue. **Distribution**: East and west coasts of the North Atlantic; winters in the south, up to the Gulf of Mexico and Senegal

The French have an evocative name for the northern gannet—*Fou de Bassan*, literally, Bassan's fool. The expression refers to the seabird's daredevil vertical dives for fish and other prey, and to Bass Rock, the world's greatest rock gannetry. The mating ground for at least 40,000 pairs of gannets, the island is located off the east coast of Scotland.

In North America, round about February and March, depending on the vagaries of wind and weather, adult gannets begin to dream of remote islands and sheer cliffs. These hardy adventurers have spent the winter months on the open ocean, and now a whopping 210,000 pairs—50,000 from the west coast of the great ocean and 160,000 from the east—set a course for one of their six colonies on this side of the Atlantic.

Denise and I have visited the well-known colony on Bonaventure Island in Quebec many times. The first time we saw it, many years ago, was on a camping trip to the Gaspe Peninsula, back when we were just casual birdwatchers. Discovering this beautiful, untamed island, dedicated to love, was one of the experiences that led us to become passionate birders.

We first took a boat tour around the high cliffs of this big, bird-filled rock, then we had to take a long walk across the island to reach the colony. There are protected observatories where we could safely (for us, the observers, as well as for the birds) watch the gannets in their wild environment.

Normally the island is shrouded in fog, as though to protect the privacy of its inhabitants. But the day of our visit was clear and windy, and we felt lost between the sea and sky. There we witnessed the yearly ritual that ensures the reproduction of one of the world's most engaging species.

We could tell which birds were more experienced, because they rushed to stake out their territories on prime real estate—steep cliff ledges overlooking the sea. With younger rivals nipping at their heels, none could afford to waste time. Altercations over nesting places led to outright skirmishes, and the colony grew steadily rowdier as the day wore on.

The male gannet stakes out his nest site by pointing his bill menacingly at it, all the while performing a head-shaking routine designed to attract a female onlooker. While male gannets are monogamous, the females are generally on the flighty side, definitely not above a casual fling. The male's light blue-gray eye, circled in deep blue, always keeps a sharp lookout. If his mate gets distracted, he promptly restores her to attention by putting on a dazzling ritualized display, alternately bowing, arching his neck, lowering his head, and rustling his wings and tail extravagantly. If he notices even the slightest glance at another male or feels that she's pulled away, however discreetly, he'll nip her on the nape, prompting her to turn around contemptuously. At this point, other birds know to leave the pair alone. Something serious is afoot.

As their guttural rah-rah sounds grow in volume, the lovers face each other, breast to breast, opening and folding their mighty wings. They point their heads skyward, crisscrossing their bills and making graceful fencing movements. Their long, supple necks entwine sensuously until that moment when the submissive female shakes her head and sinks to the ground. The introductions are over; they are now ready to get down to business. Such rituals are unique to gannets and have been refined over innumerable generations. Afterward, as if to underline the serious nature of their activity, the duo meticulously preens each other, further cementing the parental bond.

The ever-attentive male brings a bouquet of seaweed plants and other scavenged gifts to his partner. She uses the material to line her nest, making it softer and more comfortable. Both parents incubate a single blue-tinged egg over a 45-day period.

As we departed, we could see, high up on the sheer cliff faces, more gannets settling down at the end of their long winter wanderings. The terrain and remote location of this island keeps the birds safe from predators, both human and otherwise. But it cannot protect them from the pollution that plagues the surrounding ocean. We can only hope that those soaring denizens of the wind and ocean can find a way to survive, so they can return year after year to their natal home, their island of love.

Northern gannets have a wingspan of about 5 3/4 feet (1.75 m).

A female northern gannet sinks to the ground, allowing her lover to mount her.

Northern gannets build their nests on high, steep cliffs overlooking the sea.

The male gannet brings his partner a bouquet of seaweed or other vegetation. She uses it, along with feathers, to line their nest.

GREAT BOWERBIRDS

Deep in the forest of northeastern Australia, in the early hours of a mist-shrouded morning, raucous and repetitive calls ring out. They sound like nothing my wife and I have ever heard before, and they instantly get our attention. We can barely glimpse their source, a bird whose drab plumage blends into the brownish gray background. Moments later, its undulating flight reveals its identity. It was no less than a great bowerbird, arguably the most original of all avian species. Although it isn't birders he is trying to attract, I nevertheless pick up my cameras and we follow him, thrilled to photograph this unique suitor in the wild.

These pigeon-sized birds owe their name to the intricate, often garishly decorated structures that they build. The urge to nest has nothing to do with it; the bowers are specifically designed to be stage sets where the males can strut about and vocalize to entice females. Bowers themselves come in several basic shapes, the avenue and maypole varieties being the best known. The former features a tunnel-like avenue, and the latter, a display perch.

The sexes are differentiated only by the lilac-pink crest feathers, which are more abundant in males and spread out like a fan during courtship displays. The male we see is heading for his mating territory, already staked out in years past and housing an array of his own splendid bowers to show for it. Some of the structures have been damaged by bad weather, but those still intact clearly attest to the remarkable skills of this avian architect-cum-Casanova. Their location, too, reflects the builder's genius. The bird has shrewdly placed them in a secluded area, protected by a few hundred square yards of surrounding space, the better to keep potential rivals at bay.

He's now hard at work building a new bower, twig by twig. Before long, he erects a platform measuring roughly 3 inches (8 cm) high by 5 feet long by 8 feet deep (1.5 by 2.5 m). Next, two robust, 10-inch-thick (25-cm) walls of sticks go up, each 14 inches (35 cm) high by 18 inches (45 cm) long. These frame the platform and support an elaborate canopy worthy of a society wedding. Made of twigs and shrubs, the canopy also conceals the bower from predators' hungry eyes.

Now comes the fun part—decorating the tunnel-like vestibule (an "avenue" to the scientists), which is arranged in a north-south direction. Great bowerbirds love flashy objects, and our hero is no different, adorning his pad with an impressive

CHARACTERISTICS

Great bowerbird (*Chlamydera nuchalis*): Dull beige, with pinkish cast; pink nape during nuptial display. **Distribution**: Northern Australia

Bowerbirds belong to the family Ptilonorhynchidae, which comprises 19 species. Nine breed exclusively in New Guinea, 8—including the great bowerbird—live in Australia, and the remaining 2 species are found in both regions.

These photos show typical avenue bowers. The picture on the left shows a platform adorned with all-white decorative items.

selection of colorful items: fruits, flowers, tree leaves, brilliant stones, snake scales, seashells, corals—whatever he can find in his own back yard or steal from a rival's bower. Like a connoisseur, he arranges his art collection according to museum criteria—by category, shape, and color. These days, it's not uncommon to see shards of broken glass, plastic cups, strips of ribbon, or other household knickknacks amid the treasure trove—a few perhaps pilfered straight out of some human's kitchen! Many bowerbirds go even further in their decorative zeal, using their beaks to smear sticky saliva, fresco-style, on the walls inside their bowers. It's hard to believe that the entire construction is the work of a single bird!

Feeling pleased as punch with the final result, our architect is now ready for the seduction scene. He strikes a smoldering pose at the north end of his jazzily decorated bower—beak ajar, revealing a tantalizing bit of tongue—and waits for a willing female victim to appear. No sooner has one turned up than the local males straighten their postures like robots, their necks extended, lilac-pink crests spiked up, and beaks coated with gleaming saliva. Everyone looks his best, anxious for the beauty to visit *his* brand-new abode.

She flits about between bowers before making her choice. She stops by our hero's quarters. She allows him to approach, and the two disappear inside the tunnel to consummate their relationship in private.

A short while later, the female emerges and flies off into a nearby tree. There, she'll hastily assemble a cuplike nest—usually in a fork—and take control of family-related duties.

Our male, finding himself a bachelor all over again, returns to his luxurious apartments, where he'll go on fussing over his art collections, rearranging his *objets d'art* this way and that, waiting for other beauties to arrive. And of course they, too, will be dazzled by all those glitzy baubles, to say nothing of Casanova's slick manners.

ATLANTIC PUFFINS

Some people affectionately call this bird of the North Atlantic coastal regions the "little friar of the Arctic" because of the way it flies with its feet together; those feet remind them of hands folded in prayer. Others see the bird in a different light, labeling it the "sea parrot" or "clown of the sea" because of its brightly colored bill, clownlike face, and waddling walk. Its expressive eyes, set off by its white face, have melted many a heart. It should come as no surprise then that this charmer is the favorite of many birders.

I too felt the desire to see them up close and hoped to take some interesting photos of them. Maine is the southernmost puffin nesting and breeding location and the one closest to my home, so I made a boat trip to Machias Seal Island, located in the Gulf of Maine. My main goal was to observe and understand the birds' different behaviors, because this bird is not only cute and endearing, but also unique.

About the size of a pigeon, the puffin is a member of the family *Alcidae*. It does not have the equivalent of thumbs, but it does have webbed "fingers" attached to short legs that are set far back toward its posterior. This morphology makes its carriage rather stiff compared to other web-footed birds. In winter, puffins live on the open ocean and travel in small groups without ever returning to land. Their prolonged and mysterious absences can last up to seven months.

Then one day, perhaps as memories of the puffins' past loves bubble back to the surface of their minds, they begin to gather along the coast of Maine.

That's when one can see them by the hundreds—even thousands—floating in tight ranks on the waves. Soon after joining the assembly, the more exuberant ones, excited by all the noise and agitation, are en route to their favorite piece of terra firma.

Puffins are paired for life and show a great sense of fidelity, not only toward each other but also to the breeding colony and even their nest site, where the couple reinitiate their intense courtship each year. As the first notes of their love songs begin to sound, males and females don their wedding outfits. Their yellow feet turn bright red. Their bills grow larger and become vivid red, yellow, orange, and blue—colors that allow other puffins to recognize each individual's social rank and level of sexual maturity. The beauty of the bill seems to be the main attraction for both male and female. (At summer's end, when the time to return to the ocean approaches, the colorful sheath of the beak is shed and replaced by a plain one.)

With their strong black claws and beaks, they frenetically dig a 5-foot-long (1.5-meter-long) tunnel that culminates in a nuptial chamber. The couple's courtship takes place on the ground in front of their burrow, but being true seabirds, they take to the sea to copulate. In fact, the conjugal act takes place while the couple surfs on the crest of a wave.

Then the couple returns to land, where Mrs. Puffin lays her eggs in their sandy burrow. For 39 days she incubates them, while her beau stands guard at the entrance to the burrow and makes frequent trips to his fishing grounds. The latter can be an extremely risky mission, because the puffin's

CHARACTERISTICS
Atlantic puffin (*Fratercula arctica*): Black and white plumage; large gaudy bill. **Distribution**: Both sides of the North Atlantic

Facing page: When a puffin goes courting, his bill grows larger, becoming vivid red, yellow, orange, and blue. These colors allow others to recognize his social rank and level of sexual maturity.

path can cross that of great black-backed gulls and great skuas. These vicious kleptoparasites steal food from other birds and have no qualms about killing puffins, if need be. In order to confuse and distract their enemies, the astute puffins take off by tens or hundreds in every direction and at rapid speed. At the same time, other groups, with their black and white feathers stuck tight to their bodies, dive into the water, reaching speeds of up to 12 miles (20 km) an hour with the aid of their short, powerful wings. Swimming underwater and using their webbed feet as rudders, the sharp spines inside their beaks trap five or six wriggling victims, and the birds emerge from the water with their familiar silvery mustachios.

This amusing image stays on our minds even after the puffins go back out, for months on end, on the open ocean. Then again one day, the call of the mating instinct takes control, and with thousands of their peers, they head back to Machias Seal Island and the other great puffin colonies, which work their age-old magic and rekindle in the birds the spark of love.

Each year, a deep, instinctual urge pulls the puffins back to their natal islands. For the puffins shown here, that is Machias Seal Island in the Gulf of Maine.

The Return of the Puffins

Between the seventeenth and nineteenth centuries, people liked puffins for more than just their cute appearance. The puffins in the Gulf of Maine were killed for their meat and for their feathers, which adorned ladies' hats. Their eggs were also gathered for food. In addition, large populations of aggressive gulls, especially the great black-backed gull, and other predators invaded these islands and almost eliminated the puffins here. By 1902, only one pair remained on one island.

For generations, the little friars refused to return to the small islands situated on the United States–Canada border. Over the years, various strategies were tried to lure the puffins back, but for a long time nothing succeeded. Finally, one of the actions that did help was the National Audubon Society's Project Puffin, initiated in 1973. Very young birds from flocks in other parts of the world were brought to the area and reared there, with the hopes that after they had fledged, they would return to their adopted natal islands to breed. Craftily planted decoys, scattered at random, convinced the naturally gregarious birds that they could safely return.

And, happily, over time, the puffins did come home. Today, puffin populations are thriving in the gulf.

Puffins are naturally gregarious and social, but also monogamous.

The Atlantic puffin's stocky build and short legs, set far back toward its posterior, give it an awkward carriage on land. But its body is well adapted for the seven months a year it lives completely at sea.

A puffin goes a-courting.

AMERICAN WHITE PELICANS

The pelican's impressively huge orange bill makes it a consummate fisherman.

CHARACTERISTICS
American White Pelican (*Pelecanus erythrorhynchos*): Entirely white except for black wingtips; long orange bill with a pouch. **Distribution**: From southwestern Canada to southern California; winters from the southern United States to Guatemala

As soon as it's spotted, a school of carp is instantly scooped up by an armada of oversized beaks. As a sign of obvious pride after a good catch—and as a signal of victory—all the pelicans raise their wings above their backs in sort of feathered high-fives. Once they've eaten their fill, the snowy white gluttons indulge in a preening session before dozing off for a post-prandial snooze.

Roaming through California, visiting wildlife refuges, reserves, sanctuaries, and parks one after the other, we came to a small freshwater lake where, to our surprise, white pelicans gathered in numbers and were demonstrating their famous group-fishing habit. Not bothered by our presence, they also lingered on sandy islets where we could observe their courtship and mating very well, albeit discreetly.

After waking up, an uninhibited female approached the comfortable males and shook a tail feather, parading in front of them. Tantalized by the bold beauty, one of the males made it clear that he was more than willing. Then other excitable males followed suit, and, inevitably, disputes broke out. In order to impress both rivals and the lovely one, each male stretched out his neck and then, with theatrical aplomb, pointed his spectacular bill-cum-pouch heavenward. Individual conflicts are mainly a matter of showboating, and a resolution was quickly arranged, thanks to the incontestable supremacy of the most imposing individual.

Without further ado, the happy couple withdrew. The confident victor immediately tried to straddle the female who, with a quick feint, ducked under the water and escaped. "Calm down, my dear," she seemed to say. "First, let's go to the nesting area, and after that. . .well, we'll see." Slightly disconcerted, the gallant realized a little too late that his newfound paramour had a strong will and love at first sight may not be all it's cracked up to be.

As he got closer to the colony, the impetuous Don Juan saw that all his companions had already perfected the role of master of seduction. They floated by in collective squadrons, calling out to the females with curious grunts and even attempting to parade on land in clumsy disarray. Back on the water, they formed a circle and then, in unison, all pointed their bills skyward.

In order to see how the watching females would react to their gymnastic performance, the males—their eyes are bright red at this point—gazed into the pretty faces of the females. Finally won over, each female approached her Romeo, who was already hard at work driving away potential rivals. Each lucky winner proudly promenaded with his prize. On dry land he walked with a happy wiggle, spread his wings, and stretched his neck with the beak pointing downward.

The matchmaking concluded, the couple set off to pick a spot for nest-building. After serious searching, the fiancée made up her mind and indicated the place she'd chosen by clearing it off with the tip of her bill. After that, she sank low on the ground and invited the male to share the delights of mating. Afterward, no doubt hopeful that more coupling is on the offing, he filled his huge beak-pouch with twigs and grasses that his mate painstakingly arranged inside the nest. Both parents share brooding responsibilities for the 30 or so days it takes to incubate their eggs, and the young, impetuous lover would become a consummate family man.

But despite the imperative call of love and family, there was also the call of the greater pelican community. Pelican life centers around the society of the group, so we were sure our hero would still get back to the company of his buddies and their fishing expeditions.

A female pelican seduces a male into leaving his buddies for a rendezvous on the water.

Pelican life revolves around the group.

A European white pelican stares back.

Male pelicans will flex their wings and strut (as best as sea birds can) to impress potential mates.

American white pelicans demonstrate their group fishing technique.

PURPLE SWAMPHENS

Unlike purple swamphens in other parts of the world, those in New Zealand lay their eggs in large communal nests.

Most members of the family *Rallidae*, the purple swamphens of Africa, India, and southern Europe, lead fairly traditional family and sex lives. Both mating partners are monogamous and share the responsibility of raising their offspring.

However, it's quite a different story with the pukeko, the New Zealand–based representative of the family.

Denise and I had seen purple swamphens in Europe, Africa, and India. In the United States, we found the smaller but beautiful American purple swamphen. But the New Zealand swamphen's extravagant behavior especially interested me, since I was writing a book on unusual bird courtship and "love behaviors."

Purple swamphens are relatively common in New Zealand and are not hard to see. Found on both islands, they inhabit wetlands, estuaries, short damp pastures, and even in parks, where they live in extended families and are quite obvious. Visiting these birds' swampy haunts, which in some places are heated by sulfur-emitting holes in the ground, known as fumaroles, we got an up-close view of their unusual groupings—avian communes, if you will. Although the Asian populations of swamphens also live in groups, New Zealand's groups are the only ones in which anything seems to go and where everything is shared—including mates.

Two main types of purple-swamphen communes draw birders like us and curiosity seekers visiting New Zealand. Some communes are a short-lived mixed bag of vagabond types in which near anarchy reigns. A number of handsome dominant males come together, and wild sexual promiscuity is sublimated, at least temporarily. But since these males are naturally aggressive and incapable of restraining their sexual impulses, sooner or later the group will be destabilized and break up.

Other individuals seek out company that is more stable, but that still encourages liberal, easygoing ways. Longer lasting, these polygamous groupings usually number a dozen or so birds, most of them male. The small band of libidinous adults is accompanied by a half dozen assistants—young males and females from previous broods. Until these helpers are old enough to participate in the sexual activity, they handle a number of tasks, but are primarily responsible for care of the chicks. And as the little ones grow, they get quite an eyeful watching the variety of activities that take place between the adults.

Nothing appears to be off limits, no matter what the age or sex. The young ones undoubtedly notice the incestuous relations and the homosexual activities. (They would never see such things in swamphen families elsewhere in the world; these sexual behaviors are unique to their New Zealand subspecies.) But soon they discern a scale of pleasure. Little by little, they realize that nothing is perfect, even in a well-organized collective. As usually happens in communal situations, avian or otherwise, discussion and debate can get stormy before members of the group finally agree on their respective privileges and duties. This becomes

CHARACTERISTICS

Purple swamphen (*Porphyrio porphyrio* [subspecies *melanotus*]). Bright red beak with shield; purplish underparts with black above; visible white undertail coverts; 29 $^1/2$ to 34 inches (75 to 86 cm).
Distribution: Subspecies exclusive to New Zealand

evident when several males want to mate with the same female and a small riot erupts. There's a swamphen pecking order in place among the males, and it's rigidly enforced whenever some young bird gets a little too obstreperous.

Female social status is constantly reassessed. Which bird will dominate among the already dominant females? Each assumes that she can enjoy as many partners as possible before relinquishing her place to another, who seems just as confident about her own prerogatives. Once impregnated, they take turns laying their eggs in the common nest, which sometimes has two depressions. After the chicks hatch, all group members take care of the newborns and, by example, demonstrate the rules of the commune into which they were born.

Thus in New Zealand the swamphen's traditionally privileged, individualistic lifestyle has unexpectedly been replaced by a kind of collectivism. Specialists explain this transformation by pointing out that habitat erosion has forced the swamphens to sacrifice their individualistic ways. It seems only fair, then, that the members of the communes should receive something in return. Perhaps living in a group isn't so bad if it's one with so few sexual taboos!

Purple swamphens sport purplish underbodies and black upper bodies, along with bright red beaks.

With its long legs and toes, the purple swamphen, or pukeko, of New Zealand is well adapted to its swampy habitat.

New Zealand's Second Swamphen

New Zealand's other swamphen species is not nearly so numerous or libidinous as its free-wheeling cousin, the pukeko. The takahe (*Porphyrio mantelli* [subspecies *Notornis*]), at 25 inches (63 cm) tall, is the largest living rallid. Over the centuries, the flightless birds were easy targets for hunters and mammals. Now there are only about 190 birds left: 150 in the isolated Fiordland alpine grasslands and 40 dispersed on four small islands, where they have been introduced and are protected. The goal now is to increase the population to 500 birds.

Unlike the pukeko, the takahe are monogamous and stay together for life, forming permanent pair-bonds. The female lays two eggs that both parents incubate. The young leave nest soon after hatching.

The takahe is endangered, and fewer than 200 remain in New Zealand.

ANHINGAS

A female anhinga, distinguished from the male by her buff head and neck, throws back her head in a deep, guttural cry of ecstasy.

In the heart of an inhospitable Everglades bayou some very curious contortions taking place on a large branch draw our attention. Soon my wife and I see a pointy-beaked head, followed by an extremely long S-shaped black neck. The black body culminates in a long fanlike tail that shimmers in invitation and anticipation. From a distance, another long neck attached to a buff-colored breast soon responds to the overture.

The response excites the first bird, a male, even more, and he stretches his neck out still further, while his wings move in slow, undulating motions. Monogamous, like most bird couples, the two anhingas renew their vows season after season. Sometimes even the younger anhingas, fresh out of adolescence, can feel the first stirrings of desire at the mere sight of members of the opposite sex. Clearly, they like what they see.

We're dressed in camouflage suits, the better to observe the unusual behavior of these 40-inch long (1 m) fishers. These waterbirds of the South are venerated by the Amazon Indians, who gave the accomplished fish swallowers their name.

The male we're observing wants a better view of the female's graceful wings spread out wide in the sun. So, holding on by his beak, he pulls himself up a little higher. Suddenly, just as they are enjoying the preliminaries, the two winged creatures vanish beneath the water. Having mastered the art of regulating the air under their feathers centuries ago, they also instinctively know at what point gentle touches take on a more intimate connotation. I try to picture them under the water's surface: They greet and admire each other, then initiate a series of gracious dancelike movements. Next, feeling breathless, they burst through the water's surface, their snakelike necks leading the way, noisily sucking in oxygen.

With astonishing dexterity, each bird shows off a fine catch, gives itself a congratulatory flourish, and then flips the fish in the air before swallowing it headfirst. After that, the anhingas make sharp, loud cries, each claiming victory in a symbolic duel where there are no losers. The private rituals continue, then suddenly stop.

Unlike other waterbirds, anhingas are unable to waterproof their plumes. So they have no choice but to regularly halt their amorous byplay or underwater fishing expeditions and spend a great deal of time drying out. The upside to this frustrating interruption of activity is that the stifling heat of the day chases away teeming hordes of parasites.

Once the intermission is over, it's time again for intimacy. To enhance their seductiveness, the anhingas preen for a while and then silently return to urgent business. The excited male approaches the female for copulation, first offering her a gift—usually a small branch—before gently grasping her beak. Without fail, the mating ritual of the so-called snakebird elegantly climaxes with slow, undulating movements. An expandable throat pouch, which will serve as a food hamper for their future offspring, swells under the throat and gives their cries a deep, guttural sound that reflects this moment of warm intimacy.

CHARACTERISTICS

Anhinga (*Anhinga anhinga*): Male: Black body and head with a tapered bill; disproportionately long neck; furrowed white wings. Female: Neck and breast buff; rest of body similar to the male.
Distribution: Southeastern United States, Central America, and South America

Possessive and territorial, the male is primed to defend the couple's space. Thus, he ensures they have the peace necessary for the building of their haven—high up on a branch that predators cannot reach. Construction of the large, flat nest is initiated by the male, but completed by the hen, who uses the great quantity of material he brings to her. Always located above the water, the nest will be renovated over many years, all the while respecting the territorial boundaries worked out with the seven or eight other couples that also inhabit the neighborhood. The anhinga is a sociable bird and doesn't mind having egrets and herons living next door, too.

With fewer domestic duties than his mate, the male takes flight on ascending air currents. He soars further and further upward in tighter and tighter circles until we can no longer see him, while back at the nest the hen watches over five pretty little greenish blue eggs. But not to worry, the male is always ready to fly home if his mate sounds the alarm. Should an intruder appear, the male anhinga, high in the sky, folds his wings and drops like a dive-bomber on any creature—no matter how big—that threatens his family.

The male is never reluctant to replace his better half on egg patrol and, following tradition, keeps the eggs at the right temperature with his warm, webbed feet. Many dangers lurk in the swamp, and eventually he will be in charge of defending not only his mate, but also their tiny-beaked cotton balls.

The chance to observe the feathered serpent in mating season is a long-awaited gift. After this precious time with the bird, I understand the passion felt by its many admirers and why it is that they variously call it the Grecian lady, the snakebird, and the black-bellied darter. But as we leave the forest, one name haunts me, an enigmatic name inherited from a language that, alas, like so many other cultural treasures, is dying: *Anhinga*.

A male anhinga has a black body and head, plus the needle-like beak; long, S-shaped neck; and white furrowed wings shared by both sexes.

Baby anhingas may resemble beaked cotton balls, but their snakelike necks are clearly evident.

A female anhinga sounds her cry.

A male anhinga swallows his catch headfirst.

HAMERKOPS

A hamerkop strikes a seductive pose to entice its mate.

There lives in Africa an eccentric, extravagantly assembled bird that almost seems to defy classification. Even DNA testing, which allows us to identify and classify living creatures, doesn't much clarify matters, suggesting only that the hamerkop lies somewhere between the heron and the flamingo on the taxonomic scale. The French, with their romantic bent, call the bird *ombrette* (shadowy), referring to the hamerkop's dark plumage. On the other hand, the more pragmatic Dutch and English were struck by the way its beak is counterbalanced by a massive crest. No matter what name we use, the hamerkop seems to have borrowed parts of its anatomy from a number of other species, coming up with a form so unique that the experts throw up their hands. Biologists have assigned it a family all its own—*Scopus umbretta*.

This jet-setting species, with its taste for frequent house-swapping and free-for-all orgies, has spread throughout much of Africa, where it is now omnipresent.

Sometimes there are circumstances that entice us to do things that we might not have done otherwise. Long ago, I had a colleague from Senegal, an intern who had come to Montreal to study. He and his wife had liked the city and Montrealers, and my wife and I got to know them well. Many years later, I met up with him at a conference, and he invited us for a visit in his country.

That is how we came to be in east Africa, with two very nice Wallof guides, enjoying the sight of this amazing hamerkop. While we watched the weird-looking bird, our guide, Ass Ndiaye, explained its peculiar behavior. The bird not only looks funny but also acts funny.

The hamerkop is skilled in the art of smoke and mirrors. The male will even invent fake orgies, which we suspect are planned to maintain matrimonial interest and during which he simulates the sex act without actually going all the way. "Anything goes," he seems to be telling us.

The male gives the first signal by flapping his wings, raising and lowering his crest toward his inamorata, and departing on a suggestive flight accompanied by enticing calls. The female, however, will not get her hopes up too soon, for this past master of creating great expectations is often simply spicing up a dress rehearsal. After all, he feels no compunction about abandoning a fiancée if she appears a little too eager. But if, on the other hand, this is a real hormonal upsurge—which can occur anytime of the year—then nothing can stop him and his mate from consummating their torrid passion. In a cascade of acrobatic maneuvers, the game of "101 positions" gets under way. Female on top, male beneath; reversed positions or more classic ones. But their cloacae never meet, except for that much anticipated moment when they know they're ready to procreate.

CHARACTERISTICS

Hamerkop (*Scopus umbretta*): Rich sepia brown body; beak and feet black; crest at back of head; about 20 inches (50 cm) tall. **Distribution**: Central to southern Africa, Madagascar

Hamerkops are also master builders. Completely unreasonable, megalomaniac, compulsive, and unable to sit still, the hamerkop couple will work together for up to six weeks on what is always a joint project. They can't stop building ever larger and more complex edifices with never-ending architectural modifications. As soon as one exceptional construction has been finished, the couple starts work on another, apparently without any consideration for real nesting needs. Many of these habitats remain unfinished for reasons that are unclear, but the largest ones—which can weigh 100 times the weight of the bird and are capable of bearing a man's weight—are reused year after year.

In certain regions where neighborliness reigns, a small community helps out with the hamerkop couple's project. The hamerkops are so busy building that they don't have time for surveillance, and so a crowd of squatters—a mix of mammals and reptiles along with other large birds—infiltrates their luxury condos.

The most remarkable of these buildings is made from thousands of objects; some comprise more than 8,000. Just about anything that's not tied down, from the most unusual materials to everyday items—as long as they're transportable to one or the other of the birds' baroque building sites—may find their way into a hamerkop nest.

How do such fanciful ideas emerge from a bird-brain? Are we dealing with some sort of compulsive collectors who need to possess anything and everything that they find beautiful, perhaps to compensate for their own less than handsome appearance? Or maybe they have instinctively found an outlet for their strong sexual impulses. Or is this behavior simply a strange manifestation of the single-mindedness of the hammerhead? To this day, no one knows for certain.

Hamerkops are masterful—and obsessive—builders. They can't stop constructing ever larger and more complex edifices—structures that far exceed the size needed for a nest. As soon as one project is done, the hamerkop couple will immediately begin another.

The name hamerkop, or "hammer head," reflects the way this African bird's long, narrow beak is counterbalanced by a massive crest.

OSPREYS

An osprey returns to its mate in the couple's love nest.

The osprey's adventure begins early in March either in Colombia, Brazil, or—less frequently—the West Indies, when the solitary raptor, soon joined by a number of his peers, starts to feel the reproductive urge. Lured by rising air currents, he yields to the call of the North, climbing to such heights that the birdwatcher loses track of him. Then, gently, the bird lets his feathered sails carry him beyond the clouds, heading back to the place of his birth.

In the case of the ospreys we saw and photographed, that birthplace and breeding ground was on Florida's Sanibel Island, in the J. N. "Ding" Darling National Wildlife Refuge. The ospreys usually like to breed near large bodies of water, rivers, or shallow lakes—anywhere fish, their cuisine of choice, are abundant.

As soon as he arrives, the male osprey reclaims his breeding ground, patrolling the area and announcing his presence with piercing cries. He then sets about repairing the massive nest that he and his mate used in previous seasons. Made of twigs, this architectural marvel often exceeds 5 feet (1.5 m) in diameter. The ospreys build on any spot that is alongside water and out of reach of land predators—from tall trees and rock pinnacles to electrical towers and utility poles. If they cannot take the same nest of the last season, they will build a new one in the same neighborhood.

When the female arrives, she too gets busy, lining the nest with brightly colored moss, twigs, and bark. It's the beginning of a relationship during which the partners will get reacquainted. They size each other up, and, finally, either get together or go their separate ways. Comfortably ensconced in her nest, the female, whose chief concern is that her future little ones be well fed, keeps a keen eye on her betrothed's skills as a provider. She is very demanding and requires that he supply a minimum of two or three substantial fish every day. Any suitor who cannot meet this requirement could be jilted in favor of a more talented and experienced male. Most of the ospreys stay together for a lifetime, but occasionally divorces happen.

The first mating attempts occur early in the morning. The male delicately grasps the back of the consenting female with his talons while vigorously flapping his wings. These heady couplings are repeated more than 20 times a day for at least three weeks—far more frequently, of course, than reproduction actually requires. Conjugal duty is one thing, but when it's pleasurable at the same time, why not?

A younger osprey couple will be more reserved, not because they lack desire, but rather because a young male will often hesitate before expending so much energy to satisfy the desires of an unknown beauty who could easily drop him whenever it suits her. Males who've been around, who are cunning, and know how to take advantage of any situation, offer numerous tasty treats in order to acquire exclusive mating rights from the female when she is most fertile and in the best position to produce

CHARACTERISTICS
Osprey (*Pandion haliaetus*): 17 to 24^1/2 inches (43 to 62 cm); dark brown or gray above with a white chin and underbody; dark band across the eyes; brown star on top of the head. **Distribution**: Tropical and temperate regions of all the continents

healthy offspring. A successful approach will depend to some extent on temperament and circumstance, but above all on fishing skills.

Although monogamous by nature, some especially ambitious males take over nearby nests and handle the care and feeding of *two* females. The bonus is that they also get to satisfy both females' voracious sexual appetites. Such is the power of the pheromone!

Soon, the ospreys fall into a routine common to many winged couples: the hen handles the job of incubation, which lasts 35 to 40 days, while the male spends his time going back and forth between the nest and his favorite fishing spot. Greeted by approving screeches, he hands over his catch to the hen, who quickly rips it apart for her young. From

time to time, she leaves the nest herself to savor a tender trout filet in peace and quiet. This allows the male the chance to experience the joys and obligations of being the babysitter. After the sixth week of parental care, even the fittest companion begins to show signs of fatigue, finding it more and more difficult to meet the insatiable feeding demands of the small gluttons. Showing a little sympathy for the first time since her arrival in the reproduction area, milady deigns to help with the fishing.

One day, when they've made it to adulthood, the former nestlings will join the adults on their southerly migration. Paying careful attention, they will memorize the long route that they will later follow on the return trip to the land where the ospreys unite.

An osprey takes flight with a freshly caught fish, perhaps a gift to its beloved.

Ospreys build their nests near water—anywhere fish, their food of choice, is abundant—and up high, out of reach of predators.

When mating, the male osprey delicately grasps the back of the consenting female with his talons and vigorously flaps his wings.

A male osprey dives into the water after a fish. In the osprey world, the male must be a good provider to get the girl.

An osprey stands poised on a branch, studying the water for its next catch.

MOURNING DOVES

In any language, the cooing and soft moaning of doves, part gentle laughter and part melancholic sadness, are associated with love. Even today, human lovebirds see in these birds' comportment proof that love and fidelity can exist.

Some shopkeepers really know how to attract customers. Entering a splendid jewelry shop recently, I was greeted by cooing and joyful clucking. Lively and perfectly at home, a pair of ringed turtledoves invited me to spend a while with them. Completely at ease amid the precious stones in this beautiful boutique, the pair was a reminder that their species now exists only in captivity. A long time ago, somewhere in Egypt, the ancestors of these gracious doves lost their freedom. Smaller, slimmer, and more elegant than the familiar pigeon, ringed turtledoves have acquired, perhaps as a result of domestication, their more refined ways along with the sensual, muted voice that we know so well. These two talked to each other languorously, then broke into cascades of apparent laughter.

In the shop, a window was open, and I could just make out some gentle whispers from outside. There, a couple of wild mourning doves—the only species of dove still living wild—were gossiping. On the male's chest I saw a pink iridescent patch, while the female sported one that was greenish.

A little farther away, perched straight up, a single male tirelessly repeated a brooding lament that only a companion could dissipate. With throat feathers all puffed up, he voiced his sad refrain. In the distance, a gentler voice finally responded. As the pretty female approached, the male immediately sprang from his perch and noisily flapped his wings. I could imagine his heart thumping with hope. He affected a number of spiraling dives in the air, gaining altitude before each descent.

Won over, the gracious beauty approached, seized the beak of her would-be suitor, and used provocative movements to show him she was interested. Reassured, the chosen one cooed and made it clear that he was eager to begin building her a cozy nest. What followed were wing flaps of approval and tender nudges ending in a mutual grooming session, with the ever-so-subtle touches that sealed the engagement.

Once a lovely lady consents to a suitor, she waits while her valiant knight goes out to find the very best building materials. The mourning doves' nesting places are isolated and sometimes divided into individual "condos"—a few nests in the same tree. The male will deliver twigs and small branches one by one, depositing them delicately from behind her, never from the front. Is this excessive shyness, calculated effect, or refinement in both gesture and sentiment? No one has yet pierced the mystery.

Finally, perked up by his own audacity, he will dare to initiate the business that will make or break

CHARACTERISTICS

Mourning dove (*Zenaida macroura*). Smaller than the pigeon; grayish and bronze; pointed tail bordered with white outer edges; languorous and mournful song. **Distribution**: From southern Canada to Panama and the West Indies

all that he has accomplished so far: he gently climbs on the back of his willing partner.

With the appearance of one or two white eggs, the parents follow the age-old incubation ritual. The male is on duty from nine to five for daytime incubation, and perhaps to show his generosity, he allows the hen the privilege of spending the night with the hatchlings. Shift changes are established according to a schedule that never ceases to fascinate birdwatchers. As soon as the chicks appear, the crop of each parent—stimulated by hormones similar to those of mammals—secretes rich "pigeon milk." High in proteins and fat, this treat is the chicks' only food for their first three days. It gives mourning doves one of the fastest growth rates of any avian species.

When the young ones are ready to face the challenge of independent living, they will leave to join groups of friends. The parents, encouraged by the success of their first amours, will begin to raise a second family.

As for ringed turtledoves, like those in the jewelry shop, in one year they will often raise up to eight clutches in their comfy indoor nests. Alas, for some species, the saying "free as a bird" doesn't always apply.

Common throughout North America, mourning doves are smaller than pigeons and are light gray or bronzish in color.

The ringed turtledove bears a small black ring of plummage running around the back of its neck.

Mourning doves have pointed tails edged with white.

A lone mourning dove patiently awaits a potential mate.

WHITE STORKS

White storks build their nest anywhere high—in treetops, atop chimneys, on church steeples, or as here, on Roman ruins in Morocco. The nests are more than 6 1/2 feet (2 m) in height and diameter.

For my wife and me, Europe is the "mother civilization." Every time we have a chance to go there for a conference, visit friends, or simply on a vacation, we always take some time to do some birdwatching and take some photographs. This time we were in Brittany. In France, white storks belong to the landscape, and the people love the birds, because of their majestic, soaring flight and because they are symbols of fidelity, prosperity, luck, and longevity.

The white stork is one member of an extended family made up of 17 species.

First to arrive at the annual breeding area, the most experienced males return year after year to their huge nests, which can weigh up to several hundred pounds. Built on treetops, church steeples, or chimneys, these solid constructions—more than $6^1/2$ feet (2 m) in height and diameter—invariably need repairs when the storks return. Disputes and animated discussions notwithstanding, the males have to work fast: the females will arrive in a week.

As soon as the lovely ladies come home, the atmosphere changes; yesterday's belligerents put their disputes aside and rush to show themselves in the best possible light. That's when the beak clacking, wing displays, and seemingly impossible head movements begin. Partners check each other out, observing each other's elaborate choreography. The dance stops, then quickly starts all over again— both partners moving in perfect harmony, each gesture, each movement one of blooming romance and rekindled passion. The first mating will take place tonight, so seduction time is limited and the preliminaries must be brief.

The carnival-like atmosphere makes the birds giddy; the clacking of beaks, like rhythmic castanets, excites them, and soon all pairs join in the near orgiastic frenzy.

On their less-than-private nests, males and females nip at each other's beaks and neck feathers. At the height of excitation, the conqueror, like a testosterone-inflated acrobat, climbs on the back of his conquest, flaps his wings so as not to break his back and to maintain the delicate balance that any false move can upset.

Both sexes participate in nest-building repairs. Usually the male brings the material, and the female puts it in place. She also lines the nest with such materials as turf, rags, moss, or paper. (These big nests also attract other species, such as sparrows, starlings, wrens, and even rollers. These smaller birds bring material that can contribute to the stability of the big nest. And the little species also serve as alarm systems, warning the big birds of potential dangers.)

One week after many copulations the female stork starts laying three to five eggs, one every two or three days. Both parents take turns brooding, but it is always the female that incubates the eggs at night.

Although white storks have long been cited as examples of conjugal fidelity, science has disproved this cherished fancy. Bigamy—one male pairing with two females on two different nests (busy guy!)—has been recorded. In fact, the storks' true

CHARACTERISTICS
White stork (*Ciconia ciconia*): Large, slender; white body; black-tipped wings; bill and feet orangish red; black-rimmed eyes. **Distribution**: India, Africa, Europe

commitment is, as we now know, not really to each other but to their mating sites, their love nests.

For countless centuries the white stork has been a fixture in folklore as a tireless deliverer of baby children. As with most legends, it is not quite clear where the association comes from. In Germany, where the legend started, the birds returned nine months after their midsummer migration. Perhaps their return happened to coincide with the arrival of many new babies. Or perhaps the connection simply comes from the stork being a symbol of fecundity and prosperity, and babies are the symbols of the good luck and blessings they are said to bring to a household.

The eternal love triangle: a female white stork must choose between two eager suitors.

Two storks mate in their nest high above.

A stork builds its nest atop the Lupinen church in Huesca, Aragon, Spain.

White storks are easily recognized by their slender builds and long, orange legs and bills.

White storks are common in France, where this one was photographed.

The sun sets behind a stork in its nest.

GREAT EGRETS

A great egret couple searches for its lunch.

Our canoe glides along the water of a marsh bordered by the giant exposed roots typical of the mangrove. Shadows move nearby or among the trees, pirouetting like nimble ballerinas. High up on the topmost branches perch a few great egret sentinels, unmoving and watchful, reassuring the others. They recognize the canoe and especially the calm, soothing voice of our guide, Mark "Bird" Westall. (He has long been a guide here in J. N. "Ding" Darling National Wildlife Refuge, on Florida's Sanibel Island, and has played host to such notable birders as Roger Tory Peterson.)

They are truly different, these birds, so prettily called *aigreta* in the picturesque language of Provence. Great egrets, like all the egret species, are characterized by the exquisite fineness of their long, tapering feathers with their spaced-out herls, or barbs.

The mating season is at hand, that brief interlude of existence when each male must do his best to stand out and look more appealing than his neighbors in order to catch a lady's eye and attract her urge to procreate. His squawking songs sound less than erotic to the human ear. His plumage, magnificent as it is, is just like that of his peers—males and females are almost identical—merely emphasizing his anonymity.

But, our guide points out, for the last few days the rapid growth of exquisite new feathers, covering the back and neck, give each competitor a degree of individuality. Airy and sensuous, these feathery sails clearly indicate the status of each male bird during this crucial stage of the conjugal adventure.

This last-minute and temporary elegance allows an attentive female to size up the purity of the future father's genetic makeup, a key consideration for her future offspring. Since time began, these decorations have served that those most likely to ensure the survival of the species are chosen for parenthood. The breezes play among the plumes, sculpting them into myriad forms. The graceful beauty of this spectacle would melt even the hardest feminine heart. As soon as a female appears, the male's feathers stand up on end, like a lady's fan at the ball, magnifying the reflected light as the neck quivers with each stride. Such artful mastery of appearance and seduction never fails to catch the golden eye of a future conquest.

There was a time when humans too were seduced by the elegant plumes of the egret and its majestic feathers were wildly popular. Kings and queens, military officers and great beauties bedecked themselves with the egrets' feathers of love. Other people donned egret feathers, seemingly convinced that the plumes conferred on them nobility and irresistible charm on their original bearer. Such frivolous fashion statements almost destroyed these magnificent birds forever. Fortunately, in the middle of the twentieth century strict regulations finally stopped the carnage and have assured a future for these classy birds.

CHARACTERISTICS
Great egret (*Casmerodius albus* or *Ardea alba*): White plumage; yellow bill; legs and feet black.
Distribution: All continents except northern North America (Canada), northern Europe, and northern Asia

Once the female has chosen her mate, he sometimes responds with unexpected aggression. Lovely and desirable as she is, she is still an intruder on his territory and, perhaps he thinks, a threat to his bachelor freedom. He thus reacts a bit defensively at first. But he quickly gets used to her and sees the advantages of having a female about the house. Things finally quiet down, then the couple engages in some mutual preening and bill-clapping. Together they start building the nest. As it happens with many birds, the male brings the material, and the female puts it in place. This nest is where the couple usually copulates and where they will raise their family.

Great egrets are gregarious and nest in colonies, where the constant communal hubbub seems essential to their reproduction. From our canoe, we can see, situated at varying heights in the tall trees lining the marsh, the twig constructions in which the eggs will be laid. The parents will take turns watching over their brood. Soon after, the young ones, looking much like the adults, except for the delicate feathers of love, will watch their parents closely, copying their every gesture. As they grow, they will assimilate the species' secrets, until finally, grown up, they themselves will acquire the exquisite plumes.

Great egrets are gregarious and nest in colonies, where the constant communal hubbub seems essential to their reproduction.

Facing page:
An egret hunts for food among the roots of a Cyprus swamp.

A male great egret shows off its dramatic breeding plumage to attract a female mate.

Neck tucked in and legs stretched out behind, a great egret skims across the water.

Egrets favor the areas of tall grass that line the edges of lakes and marshes.

A great egret feeds its two chicks.

$\mathcal{P}$EAFOWL

For centuries, the peacock has been the uncontested champion of one of nature's most spectacular nuptial displays.

It's early morning in northern India, and the first light of day is finally appearing. At a crossroads, night watchmen at the Bharatpur Bird Sanctuary are finishing their shift. They stir up the embers of their fire and offer us a cup of steaming tea. After the handshake and head nod that seal agreements in this part of the world, the guides bring us to the narrow trail bordered with high grass, brambles, and thorns. We're entering nature's domain.

Suddenly, powerful cries can be heard, and, taken up in chorus by the echo, an alert is sounded. *Minh-ao! minh-ao!* is what our Indian friends hear; *Mayo! Mayo!* is what our Western ears hear.

To our left, a group of peafowl—those celebrated and colorful birds—rest in the branches of a huge tree. The local people call their emblematic bird the *mor mayura*.

During the day, the peacock is very much the individualist, but nightfall offers a chance to rekindle family ties. Alert and watchful, the birds have keen vision, exceptional hearing, and powerful voices, all of which ensure their safety.

In the mating season, of course, peacocks have other things on their minds. Mating is serious business, and each male returns to his private territory. He reserves a space expansive enough to allow for strutting and parading. The area must be open, the better to size up today's companions and observe tomorrow's rivals from a suitable distance. A peahen must always be greeted with proper etiquette. For centuries, the peacock has been the uncontested champion of one of nature's most spectacular nuptial displays—displays that can include gleaming and subtle tones of red, orange, ochre, brown, and black.

Who can deny that he's one of the handsomest representatives of the ornithological world? To enhance a face masked in black and white and crowned with a delicate crest, he puffs out his metallic-blue neck. A few rays of sunlight reflect on the prisms of the 150 feathers that make up his 3 1/2-foot-long (1 m) tail, or train. Soon the tail spreads open into a fan of spectacular beauty, and its owner turns around to make each part of it shimmer and rustle. The fan's bright "eyes," sometimes used to frighten an enemy, are a key element of seduction. Elevating the fan multiples the reflections on the green feathers and increases their unequalled beauty.

Bowled over by such a majestic display, the female drops to the ground. Gently covered by the male's long tail, they accomplish the final act of this unparalleled play.

Modesty is not a word in the peacock's vocabulary, and for the great showman, attending to an audience of just one admirer isn't enough. This bearer of fine genetic baggage considers himself perfectly capable of satisfying the greatest number of ladies.

CHARACTERISTICS

Peafowl (*Pavo cristatus*): Male: long multicolored train adorned with eyespots; fan-shaped crest on crown. Female: brownish; much shorter train; duller crest. **Distribution:** India, Sri Lanka; captive flocks seen throughout the world

Because there are neither referees nor impartial rules governing the situation, tensions usually escalate between rivals and disputes proliferate. This is when the peacock's cinnamon-colored wings—short, wide, rounded off, and powerful—become formidable weapons. Far more dangerous than their short foot spurs, the wings land blows that can put all but the most aggressive and experienced birds to flight. The victor takes the spoils: the female fans come running, all eager to honor the unrepentant polygamist.

Peafowl nest on the ground protected by undergrowth and scrub, usually at a woods' edge. The nest is a summary depression where the female lays five to seven creamy white eggs, which she incubates alone for 28 days. The male takes no part in the household duties—he's too busy strutting about with his other two to five wives.

Venerated by his harem, the brave and handsome peacock is also admired for his courage in meeting dangerous snakes head-on. In fact, on the trail home, we chance upon one such deadly confrontation, confirming the peacock's legendary reputation as a cobra killer.

We reach the watchmen's crackling fire after dark. Peacocks are protected in India for religious reasons, and in reverent tones the watchmen tell us of the myriad beliefs surrounding the bird-god. And in the distance, night voices can be heard: *Mayo. . . Mayo . . . .* The peacocks sound the first warning cries as the sweet moments of love subside and come to an end.

This peahen and peacock seem posed for an old-fashioned wedding portrait. Her coloring consists mainly of modest browns, while his comprises flashy, iridescent jewel tones.

About 150 feathers that make up his 3 $^{1}/_{2}$-foot-long (1 m) train.

A peahen stands before a peacock trying to attract her attention.

A peacock and peahen preen as part of their courtship ritual.

During the day, each male peacock jealously guards his own territory, but at nightfall, all of the birds gather together in trees for protection.

WOOD DUCKS

Arguably the most beautiful duck in the world, the male wood duck sports multicolored plumage, a very long crest, and a red or vermilion eye. He dons this handsome wedding garb during the mating season, from October to June.

Scientists call the wood duck *Aix sponsa,* from the Greek noun *aix* for "waterbird" and the Latin *sponsa,* "the fiancé." A fiancé he is, but a fleeting one—his commitment hardly lasts more than a single season and is based essentially on appearances.

But what appearances! Exclusive to North America, the wood duck, or woody, is undoubtedly the most beautiful duck in the world. In wedding garb from October to June, this classy, crested ladies' man relies on his exceptional good looks to attract and seduce females. The distaff side, for her part, wears plain-colored plumage, the better to camouflage herself and ensure the security of her little ones.

However, being too handsome can have a downside; in the past, the male wood duck's extraordinary colors proved almost fatal to the species. During the nineteenth century, the wood duck was a very popular target for humans, who were drawn by the beauty of its stunning feathers and the taste of its tender flesh. As a result, the species was almost wiped out. Today, it's much harder to observe the wood duck in truly wild habitat. Many of us see them only near "civilized" ponds and in parks, where their presence is an aesthetic plus. Denise and I most frequently find them in a little protected marsh near home. We are very lucky because we have many suburban areas and parks near Montreal, where nature is generous and we can find many interesting species of birds.

Sensitive to the cold, wood duck couples leave the site of their summer *amours* and head south after the first autumn frosts. During the long return trip, around the end of March and the beginning of April, the two bail out of the relationship and go their separate ways. Wood ducks are monogamous, but only for one season. It's a highly unsettling situation for the males, who far outnumber the females and therefore have limited options.

The next time the ducks come back north, it is with a new mate. Returning to the summer marsh, the new brides and grooms strengthen their union by resuming the rituals that had attracted them to each other in the first place—rituals whose subtle refinements are understood only by the participants.

Once the female has been reassured that her handsome new lover is still hers, she selects a cavity drilled by a woodpecker in a tree. (The habit of living in trees gave the wood duck its name.) Then the two rekindle the flames of passion. Proud to the point of arrogance, the male raises his superb

CHARACTERISTICS
Wood duck (*Aix sponsa*): Male: multicolored plumage; very long crest; red or vermilion eye. Female: much duller, white eye ring. **Distribution**: Southern Canada, entire United States, northern Mexico

crest, making it appear twice as big. He swaggers around, all the while turning his head from left to right. He struts his stuff, highlighting his magnificent colors and the other attributes that he and he alone possesses.

All this commotion draws curious onlookers and, as a consequence, potential rivals. The male has to keep an eye on bachelors, singletons, or mismatched males that lurk nearby, on the lookout for any opening when he is distracted. Only the most talented and vigilant will eventually have the honor of helping to perpetuate the species.

Since they nest in a cavity, their eggs don't need to be camouflaged. The female lays about a dozen glossy, unmarked white eggs, which she incubates for 27 to 37 days. It is always amazing to see the newborn ducklings, one to two days old, falling down from their nest, sometimes into the water but also sometimes onto the ground.

Based on snobbery or prudence, the wood duck practices discrimination and avoids mixed marriages; it seems wood ducks do not indulge in relations with other duck species who are less blessed by nature and would therefore compromise their legendary beauty.

The female wears plain-colored plumage, the better to camouflage herself and ensure the security of her young.

Wood ducks are monogamous, but only for a single mating season. The pair will split up when it's time to fly south for the winter.

$\mathcal{M}$ALLARDS

A male mallard soars gracefully in for a landing.

It's February on Quebec's Chateauguay River, and I'm watching mallards nip at and chase one another, stretch, dive underneath the water, resurface, slide on patches of ice, and quack up a storm. No doubt about it, the unbridled activity of this hundred or so lads and lassies is a sure sign that mating season has begun. In this particular wintering area, where city-generated heat keeps the water mostly free of ice year round, their hormonal upsurge comes earlier than those of their country cousins. Other duck species that flew to the warmer south won't return to their northern nesting areas until the end of March and the beginning of April.

Mallards number in the hundreds of millions across the wetlands of North America, Europe, and Asia. They are the best known of all wildfowl and much sought after by hunters, gourmands, and birdwatchers. They are also studied by great numbers of people, many of whom are interested in the stories concerning their sexual prowess. And there's no getting away from it: this water-fowl *does* seem to have a one-track mind. Specialized publications praise the mallard's free-wheeling sexual habits.

The mallard will mate with any other duck. In fact, it's believed to be the ancestor of all domesticated ducks. Its sexual interludes with the American black duck are so frequent that they are jeopardizing black duck reproduction and limiting its offspring. The problem is so serious that the mallard may one day be responsible for the disappearance of its cousin, whose own progeny has steadily declined.

Monogamous for a season—or for just one occasion—mallard couples live in such close proximity to others that temptation is frequent. So much exposed skin and feathers present enticing opportunities, and they easily succumb. Their great numbers encourage the formation of groups of excited males, bands of sexual predators that egg one another on in their favorite pursuit—gang bangs, to put it bluntly. Such behavior may look disconcertingly like wild, traumatizing rape to those who witness it for the first time without warning. The shaken victim of these attacks inspires pity. These acts of aggression, often perpetrated when regular female partners are away, explain why paternity is often hard to prove.

While the conscientious mothers sit on their pretty eggs, their mates get together to explore and hunt for food. These male-bonding activities are ideal opportunities for these bawdy birds to indulge in the charms of other chestnut-colored temptresses, with their cinnamon highlights and black stripes. Fooling around is epidemic, likely affecting more than half of all mallard families.

Every year, the female returns to the same nesting area, usually with her latest lover in tow. This temporary fidelity leads the poor male to

CHARACTERISTICS
Mallard (*Anas platyrhynchos*): Male: Green head; white neck ring; rusty chest. Female: Mottled brown. Both male and female: iridescent blue speculum with white borders. **Distribution**: Europe, Asia, North America, northwestern Africa

unfamiliar regions where, although disoriented, he has to defend territory that another previously established for the lovely lady. And, as you might guess, things often go badly for the transplanted lover. As freewheeling as mallard males are, they also get extremely jealous if any other bird, male or female, looks at his woman. The drake will chase, attack, and fight any intruders, not to defend the eggs, but to keep them away from her.

Mallards usually nest on the ground, but they also can set up their nursery in tree holes. The nest is made of grass, reeds, and twigs and, like those of other ducks, lined with down. The female will incubate seven to ten white eggs for 28 days. She continues to be the primary caregiver after they hatch, keeping watch over the ducklings by herself.

Upon leaving the nest, young mallards are attracted to any moving object they encounter, especially if the object in question is green or orange tinted. Their identification problems can lead to comical situations—such as when a horny youngster tries to mate with a bird of a different species that just happens to have the same colors as its parents.

Mallards have freewheeling, even licentious, ways, and while some of the birds are excessive, just as many are submissive. It should come as no surprise, then, that their squabbling and raucous parties on the half-frozen river are unlikely to end soon.

A female mallard rests in the sun, one leg tucked up beneath her wing.

Mrs. Mallard is the primary caregiver for the ducklings after they hatch and keeps watch over them by herself.

Mallards number in the hundreds of millions across the wetlands of North America, Europe, and Asia. They are the best known of all wild waterfowl.

Mallards will mate with any other duck, including black ducks. The black duck (Anas rubripes) resembles the female mallard, but it is darker and has purple speculum without white borders.

Male and female mallards are easily distinguishable. The female mallard's plumage is mainly mottled brown; the male has a sleek, emerald green head, white neck ring, and a rust-colored chest.

More than 20 years ago, on a beautiful spring afternoon, a male cardinal appeared at our Montreal bird feeder for the very first time. The colorful visitor came back the following days and seemed to want to settle in our yard. The news spread, and amateur birders flocked to the scene. Even some TV units came to film this unusual visitor from the United States.

The excitement reminded me of the narratives of the first Europeans who explored the fauna of the New World. They all wanted to bring home some samples that would amaze their friends and intrigue the scientists. The little wonder in its scarlet suit was one of the first stars to be kidnapped, and its first European appearance was in mostly Catholic Italy. The Italians, enraptured by its coloring, elevated the newcomer to the highest rank: it was proclaimed "the cardinal" because its feathers were the same scarlet as the coats of the princes of the Church. Throughout Europe, even today, the cardinal is extolled, its beauty is admired, and its rich, melodious voice is deemed worthy of the most famous concert halls.

Every spring since his first visit to our yard, the singer, displaying a brilliant red outfit with some fulvous accents, sits in the top of the biggest tree in our garden and repeats his melodious outbursts, which never fail to seduce a choosy mademoiselle. The more sedately colored, tawny females always prefer the suitors with the most sparkling plumage and divine voices. The lady sings divinely, too, and answers her lover with lovely countersinging and unambiguous, enticing behavior.

Once he has conquered her, the male is gallant. He gathers sunflower seeds from the feeder and cracks them for her. Sometimes, he catches an insect and very proudly brings it to her. She opens her beak, and he shyly delivers the offering.

Cardinals are usually monogamous, and couples are relatively faithful. But if a better singer and with even more brilliant feathers appears, the belle can't always keep herself from responding to the newcomer's charm. She might leave and join a new prince with the golden voice and the sparkling gala outfit without even saying goodbye. So our hero will not readily accept intrusions from a competitor. He will both attack his rival with his beak and increase his acrobatic antics to overshadow the other.

The triumphant lover invites his companion to choose a safe, discreet bush where they will be

CHARACTERISTICS

Northern cardinal (*Cardinalis cardinalis*): Male: brilliant red, erect crest, black patch surrounding a thick, red bill. Female: olive gray with reddish wings and crest; red bill. Bigger than a sparrow but smaller than a robin (7 $\frac{1}{2}$ to 9 inches [19 to 23 cm]). **Distribution:** Eastern Canada (Ontario and Quebec), eastern United States, Mexico

A male cardinal shows off his red colors to attract a female's eye.

able to raise a new generation. She inspects it, verifies the security of the lodging, then sets up a platform nest.

Although all the world will hear them sing of their love, cardinals are very discreet when it comes to the actual act; it is unusual to see them copulate. When she is ready, the lady crouches and raises her head and tail—an obvious to the male, who, crest erect, answers her desire. The love act is sealed with beautiful countersinging.

Depending on the abundance of provisions, the couple may have up to three clutches before the summer is over.

In the fall, the exhausted parents hurry to chase away the little ones. The prince, who had been so attentive and solicitous at the time of courtship, now imperiously forbids his companion to approach the feeders until he himself has satisfied his hunger. He raises his crest, like a crown, reminding others of his noble rank and to arouse the respect he is due.

But his regal pride is short-lived, because soon spring arrives to remind him that he has to prove himself all over again with his voice and his feathers. Because when it comes to cardinal love, it is the princess who holds the last word.

While male cardinals are brightly colored to attract mates, the female wears more subdued tones, which provide camouflage for her as she cares for her young.

The male cardinal with the most brilliant plumage and most sublime song usually gets the girl.

Burrowing Owls

A pair of burrowing owls stand guard over their domain.

It was some uneasy golfers who led me to the burrowing owls. The players had come to Florida for their favorite sport, but had become unnerved by two pairs of huge golden eyes that had been observing their less-than-impeccable strokes. Worse, the spectators, who were perched on small mounds in the middle of the course, seemed to exchange amused, understanding winks, completely interfering with the golfers' concentration.

It turned out that these onlookers were not there to critique the sport, but were guarding the entrance to their new troglodytic dwelling. All 19 subspecies of burrowing owls, including this one from Florida, hide their families in underground apartments abandoned by hares, prairie dogs, or other skilled tunnel diggers. The most enterprising ones use their forceful beaks and claws to dig their own underground corridors, 6.5 to 10 feet (two to three meters) wide, leading to a spacious chamber. When I went to observe them, I found them engaged in forceful arguments over who would get the best lots with a view of the golf course. There were even some sharp beak strokes involved.

The courtship season was in full swing for the birds, as the lovers of past seasons reunited. Burrowing owls are usually monogamous, but occasionally can be polygamous. They sometimes nest in loose colonies of 4 to 14 burrows, spaced about 45 feet (14 m) apart, and, as the saying goes, "opportunity makes the thief."

The usual seduction games had started with some mutual grooming. Then every male seemed determined to bring back to his partner the plumpest rodents, to prove to her, once more, that she had chosen the best mate. Then they started to renovate their underground dwellings, which were a bit tattered.

The copulating habits to the owl family are not often seen by humans, since they usually take place at dusk or at night. When the couples are ready for the big moment, the female crouches, humbly shivering her wings, waiting for the male to mount her. Pre- and postcopulating allopreening reinforces the relationship.

Some of the five or six pairs I saw had already mated and were nourishing six to eight little hungry ones. Burrowing owls are social birds, but single nests are as common as small colonies. They don't seem to defend territories, but might band together to fight and chase predators.

While the mothers guarded the eggs for some 30 days, the fathers demonstrated their exceptional hunting skills. Sometimes the task was more demanding and took more time than anticipated. Some females, feeling neglected, let themselves be briefly seduced by the charms of an insisting neighbor. But they were the exceptions to the rule.

Burrowing owls are fearful predators who prefer to hunt in daylight rather than at night, even if it means their attacks are not as stealthy. As a fat

CHARACTERISTICS
Burrowing owl (*Athene cunicularia*): Brown with white spots; long legs, round face, eyes lemon gold; 7 1/2 to 9 inches (19 to 25 cm) tall. **Distribution:** From western North America south to Honduras, and from Florida south to the Terra del Fuego in Chile

lizard, an agile snake, a small rodent, or a swift grasshopper moves between the rocks, the skilled huntress follows them cautiously. She keeps a respectful distance, controlling her impatience until that exact moment when a chase is the sure end in success. She preserves the silence, so that the prey is unaware of her until the moment when she sinks her sharp claws into it.

Although humans, who long to live in rich suburbs and who amuse themselves by hitting balls on green playgrounds, have transformed the owls' ancestral grassland habitat, the feathered Floridians have slowly adapted to their new setting. Often, the little owls on the golf course would catch lost balls and spirit them away. Some golfers insisted on recovering their possessions, but the wiser ones desisted in view of the birds' irritated looks.

I lingered around after the last golfer had left, observing discreetly as the lovers intimately reaffirmed their relationship by exchanging a last lizard. In the small opening of their burrow, finally reunited, the fiery look of the little burrowing owls becomes less ardent. In the distance, their night cousins have begun their mournful calls. The little cave-dwelling family members returned to their lodging and, admiring their immaculate collection of golf balls, congratulated themselves on having chosen to live on such a beautiful golf course.

A burrowing owl stands guard.

A burrowing owl stands at the entrance to its underground home. The owls are so named because they nest in tunnels that they dig themselves or that have been abandoned by hares, prairie dogs, or other animals.

A lone burrowing owl maintains a wary watch.

With a steely stare, a burrowing owl looks out for intruders.

EASTERN BLUEBIRDS

A bluebird swallows a berry while perched in a tree in the Great Smoky Mountain National Park.

The winter has just started to vanish, though some snow mounds still linger in dark corners. The call of spring is irresistible. I head toward a farm located some 10 miles north of Montreal, where on the stakes of a rustic fence, the farmer has set up some small cottages. Several even bear addresses: 1352, 1354, 1358 . . . .

The first eastern bluebirds have returned in full regalia—their bright blue feathers splendid as ever—and are proclaiming their rights as the new occupants. These bluebirds from America have the good fortune of being able to invite a fiancée to share a brand-new, spacious, five-star lodging instead of a common hollow hidden under the worm-eaten bark of a tree.

Dazzling and full of enthusiasm, the males' trills sound particularly inspired, and after a few demonstrations, an impressive number of females rush in, hoping to share the dream homes. The males are attired in vivid blue over their backs and heads; the females wear bluish gray. Together they evaluate their potential dwellings. If a belle decides to linger in the new apartment, the deal is quickly settled; a couple is formed or reestablished, and the rustic cottage becomes their little love nest. The female is the one to build or refurbish the nest, and she does it in a careless way. But since the nest is in a birdhouse or tree cavity, she does not need to be a perfectionist. She makes a cup of loosely arranged grasses and twigs, just to make the house a little more comfortable.

In years past, invasive and unscrupulous neighbors had threatened to exterminate the eastern bluebirds, so now the newlyweds are suspicious of other species and tolerate only peaceful swallow couples near their new quarters.

The nuptial parades are many. First the couple flies around, as light as butterflies. Then they flit around the nest, contemplating it. A flapping and bristling of the wings signals increasing passion. All the while, the pair exchange more and more of their characteristic sweet, melodious whistling songs.

The couple will consummate their love near the chosen nest site and may start their lovemaking even before the nest building. They will continue to copulate while the female incubates the eggs.

Love being love, they are soon sharing their home with four or five small hungry gizzards. Nested in the little cottages of the artisan farmer, the tiny bluebirds, in their brown-gray feathers streaked with white marble, have a cozy childhood. Quickly, they grow into adolescents, larger than the size of a house sparrow but smaller than a robin, and venture into the wide world. In time, they and their parents begin to make their autumn exodus to the southeastern United States, Mexico, and Central America.

When spring comes again, let's hope that the bird lovers of North America will have the pleasure of welcoming once more the charming little eastern bluebirds.

CHARACTERISTICS

Eastern bluebird (*Siala sialis*): Males are blue with chestnut-colored breasts. Females and the juveniles are a duller shade, but always tinted with blue on the wings and the tail. Adults are a little bigger than the house sparrow (6 to 7 $^1/_2$ inches; 16 to 19 cm). **Distribution:** From the south of Canada to Nicaragua

A pair of eastern blue-
birds get reacquainted
during the spring
courtship season.

Having approved of
her new house, a
female eastern blue-
bird begins building
her nest.

A melodious, whistling song marks the return of spring and the eastern bluebird to northern North America.

A bluebird holds a berry in its mouth, perhaps a gift for its mate.

About the Author

Jean Léveillé is a doctor of nuclear medicine whose passion for the world of birds led him to be bitten by the camera bug. For over fifteen years, he has contributed a regular bird column to a medical journal, and his photographs have appeared in a variety of publications. An indefatigable birdwatcher, he has traveled to the four corners of the globe—including the remotest regions—in order to capture his "identified flying objects" on film. He describes and portrays their behavior with humor and precision. He lives in Montreal, Quebec, with his wife, Denise.

Index